Taxcafe Tax Guides

Pension Magic

How to Make the Taxman Pay for Your Retirement

By Nick Braun PhD

Important Legal Notices:

Published by:
Taxcafe UK Limited
67 Milton Road
Kirkcaldy KY1 1TL
Tel: (0044) 01592 560081
Email: team@taxcafe.co.uk

7th Edition, June 2017

ISBN 9781911020196

Disclaimer
Before reading or relying on the content of this tax guide please read the disclaimer.

Pay Less Tax!

...with help from Taxcafe's unique tax guides

All products available online at

www.taxcafe.co.uk

Popular Taxcafe titles include:

- *How to Save Property Tax*
- *Using a Property Company to Save Tax*
- *How to Save Inheritance Tax*
- *Landlord Interest*
- *Salary versus Dividends*
- *Using a Company to Save Tax*
- *Small Business Tax Saving Tactics*
- *Keeping it Simple: Small Business Bookkeeping, Tax & VAT*
- *Tax Planning for Non-Residents & Non Doms*
- *Tax Saving Tactics for Salary Earners*
- *Pension Magic*
- *Isle of Man Tax Saving Guide*
- *Tax-Free Capital Gains*
- *How to Save Tax*

Disclaimer

1. This guide is intended as **general guidance** only and does NOT constitute accountancy, tax, financial, investment or other professional advice.

2. The author and Taxcafe UK Limited make no representations or warranties with respect to the accuracy or completeness of this publication and cannot accept any responsibility or liability for any loss or risk, personal or otherwise, which may arise, directly or indirectly, from reliance on information contained in this publication.

3. Please note that tax legislation, the law and practices by Government and regulatory authorities (e.g. HM Revenue & Customs) are constantly changing. We therefore recommend that for accountancy, tax, financial, investment or other professional advice, you consult a suitably qualified accountant, tax advisor, financial adviser, or other professional adviser.

4. Please also note that your personal circumstances may vary from the general examples given in this guide and your professional adviser will be able to give specific advice based on your personal circumstances.

5. This guide covers UK taxation only and any references to 'tax' or 'taxation', unless the contrary is expressly stated, refer to UK taxation only. Please note that references to the 'UK' do not include the Channel Islands or the Isle of Man. Foreign tax implications are beyond the scope of this guide.

6. All persons described in the examples in this guide are entirely fictional. Any similarities to actual persons, living or dead, or to fictional characters created by any other author, are entirely coincidental.

Dedication

Once again, to Aileen for all your love and support and to Jake, Sandy and Tilly for all the joy you bring.

About the Author & Taxcafe

Dr Nick Braun founded Taxcafe in 1999, along with his partner Aileen Smith. As the driving force behind the company, their aim is to provide affordable plain-English tax information for private individuals, business owners and professional advisors.

Over the past 17 years Taxcafe has become one of the best-known tax publishers in the UK and has won several prestigious business awards.

Nick has been a specialist tax writer since 1989, first in South Africa, where he edited the monthly *Tax Breaks* publication, and since 1999 in the UK, where he has authored several tax books including *Small Business Tax Saving Tactics* and *Salary versus Dividends*.

Nick also has a PhD in economics from the University of Glasgow, where he was awarded the prestigious William Glen scholarship and later became a Research Fellow.

Contents

Introduction

Let's get straight down to business. There is only one reason why you should put money into a pension and that is to SAVE TAX.

As a pension saver you enjoy two important tax reliefs:

- Tax relief on your contributions – what I call buying investments at a 40% discount.

- Tax-free growth – all your income and capital gains are completely tax free.

However, if maximising tax relief is your priority, as it should be, there's a lot more to it than simply putting away a fixed amount each year.

You may wish to decide *how much* to invest, making bigger or smaller pension contributions in some years or none at all.

You may wish to consider *who* makes the contributions: you, your employer, or your spouse.

You may also want to look at *when* is the best time to invest.

And, of course, you may want to know *why* you should even bother investing in a pension in the first place. For example, are pensions better than other investments like ISAs and Lifetime ISAs?

All of these important issues are addressed in this guide and I think you will be surprised by some of the results.

In Part 1 we explain how tax relief on pension contributions is calculated and how much you are allowed to invest. However, as we shall discover, calculating the maximum pension contribution you *can* make is not as important as calculating the maximum pension contribution you *should* make to maximise your tax relief.

Over 200,000 people do not claim all the tax relief to which they are entitled, so we also explain how you can make a backdated tax relief claim and avoid other common mistakes that could cost you thousands of pounds.

Pension Freedom Has Arrived

Up until recently the amount of money you could withdraw from your pension was tightly controlled. Most individuals' savings could only come out at a trickle, either through one of those universally detested annuities or something not much better called "capped drawdown".

These restrictions have now been lifted completely, giving pension savers more control over their money than they have ever had.

Once you reach the minimum retirement age (currently 55) you have complete freedom to withdraw as much or as little money as you like from your pension pot, whenever you like.

For the first time, pension savers have the ability to control their tax bills, by making big pension withdrawals in some tax years and smaller withdrawals in others.

The Government has also removed another of the major obstacles that has put people off using pensions to save for retirement. Up until recently, when you died your remaining pension savings were taxed at 55% before being passed on to certain family members.

This hefty tax charge has now been abolished and pension pots can be inherited by family members with no adverse tax penalties.

In Part 2 of the guide we explain all of the "Pension Freedom" changes and show you how to save thousands of pounds in both income tax and capital gains tax by timing your pension withdrawals carefully.

In Part 3 we show how pensions are much more powerful tax shelters than ISAs. We track two investors over a number of years and reveal that a pension saver could end up with as much as 42% more retirement income than an ISA investor.

We also explain some of the lesser known tax differences between ISAs and pensions (for example, why some dividend income is taxed inside an ISA and why your family may be better off if your money is in a pension).

The New Lifetime ISA

Those under the age of 40 can now open a "Lifetime ISA" and use it to save either for a first home or for retirement.

In Part 3 we'll tell you everything you need to know about this fantastic new saving vehicle and why some taxpayers will end up with 18% more retirement income if they use a Lifetime ISA instead of a traditional pension.

In Part 4 we look at the pros and cons of postponing and accelerating pension contributions. We show how basic-rate taxpayers – those earning under £45,000 (£43,000 in Scotland) – can increase their pension pots by 33% by delaying making pension contributions for several years.

This part of the guide also contains a fascinating case study which reveals that – even if you postpone pension contributions for several years – you will not necessarily end up one penny worse off than someone who makes pension contributions for many years.

There is one group who should always consider making pension contributions: households where the highest earner's income is between £50,000 and £60,000 and child benefit is being claimed.

Your family's child benefit payments are steadily taken away as your income rises from £50,000 to £60,000. As a result, by using pension contributions to reduce taxable income, people in this income bracket will enjoy tax relief of up to 72% or more! Full details in Part 4.

Employees, Business Owners & Landlords

In Parts 5 to 8 we look at different types of pension saver: salaried employees, company owners, self-employed business owners and landlords.

In Part 5 we explain 'auto-enrolment': the new system of compulsory pensions that has resulted in many employees enjoying a pension contribution from their employer for the first time.

Some individuals who can receive free money from their employers in the shape of a company pension contribution may decide not to take up the offer. So in this part of the guide we also publish an interesting table which shows you just how much bigger your pension pot will be if you take full advantage of the free cash your employer is offering.

Part 6 looks at salary sacrifice pensions, which can boost your pension contributions by an astonishing 34%! Salary sacrifice pensions allow you to claw back not just income tax but *national insurance* as well, including the 13.8% national insurance paid by your employer.

A salary sacrifice pension is not just a tax-efficient way to save for retirement, it is arguably the most powerful tax-saving tool available to salaried employees.

Part 7 covers company owners and directors and reveals why company pension contributions are a highly tax-efficient way to extract money from your business, following the recent increase in dividend tax rates. We also explain why getting your company to make the pension contributions is currently more tax efficient than making the contributions yourself.

Most of this guide is relevant to self-employed business owners (sole traders and the like). Some additional practical pointers are provided in Part 8 to help this group maximise their tax relief.

I've also included a chapter here for landlords. It explains how, with the help of pension contributions, you can reverse the tax increase you may suffer now that your buy-to-let mortgage interest is no longer fully tax deductible. The final chapter in Part 8 looks at the pros and cons of putting commercial property into a pension.

Finally, we get to Part 9 which, with the help of a detailed case study, answers a key family pension planning question: "Who should make the pension contributions, me or my spouse/partner?"

And in the last chapter we look at the pros and cons of opening a pension for your children or grandchildren.

I hope you find *Pension Magic* an enjoyable and interesting read.

Scope of this Guide

This guide does not cover every aspect of pension saving. The focus is *maximising tax relief*, which is the main reason people invest in the first place.

I do not cover issues like pension charges, how you should invest your money (in shares, bonds, property etc), or how to choose a pension provider. I make no excuses for these omissions. As it is, I've struggled to keep the guide to around 200 pages, focusing almost entirely on tax saving strategies. Other pension issues are all covered very well by others in the financial media.

Furthermore, all of the coverage in this guide is about defined contribution pension schemes, also known as money purchase schemes. These include personal pensions, SIPPs and their corporate equivalents. The basic idea is you (and your employer if you have one) put money in and the amount of pension income you enjoy at the end of the day depends on how well your investments perform.

All individual pensions are structured along these lines and most corporate pension schemes are moving in this direction, if they haven't done so already. There is very little discussion of defined benefit or final salary pension schemes which are becoming increasingly scarce in the private sector. If you belong to one, all I can say is, I'm jealous!

Scottish Taxpayers

The Scottish Parliament now has the power to set its own income tax rates and thresholds. Most of the information in this guide is relevant to Scottish taxpayers. However, unless stated to the contrary, all examples and calculations are based on the assumption that the taxpayer concerned is not a Scottish taxpayer.

Finally, please remember that this guide is not meant to be a substitute for proper professional advice. Before you act you should contact either a suitably qualified accountant, tax advisor, IFA or pensions expert who understands your personal circumstances.

Part 1

Putting Money In:
The Pension Contribution Rules

Chapter 1

Tax Relief on Contributions: How it's Calculated

When you make pension contributions the taxman will top up your savings by paying cash directly into your plan. Effectively for every £80 you invest, the taxman will put in an extra £20.

Why £20, you might be asking? Well your contributions are treated as having been paid out of income that has already been taxed at the basic income tax rate of 20%. The taxman is therefore refunding the income tax you've already paid.

The company that manages your pension plan – usually an insurance company or SIPP provider – will claim this money for you from the taxman and credit it to your account.

So whatever contribution you make personally, divide it by 0.80 and you'll get the total amount that is invested in your pension pot.

Example
Peter invests £4,000 in a self-invested personal pension (SIPP). After the taxman makes his top-up payment, the total amount of money Peter will have sitting in his pension pot is £5,000:

$$£4,000/0.80 = £5,000$$

Basic-rate tax relief isn't the end of the story. If Peter is a *higher-rate* taxpayer, paying tax at 40%, he'll be able to claim even more tax relief.

The Cherry on Top – Higher Rate Relief

For the 2017/18 tax year a higher-rate taxpayer is someone who earns more than £45,000 (£43,000 in Scotland).

If you are a higher-rate taxpayer the taxman will let you claim your higher-rate tax relief when you submit your tax return.

Alternatively, if you are a company employee, higher-rate tax relief can be provided immediately by reducing the tax paid on your salary via your PAYE code.

(See Chapter 4 for more information on how to claim higher-rate tax relief.)

Example
As we already know, Peter's personal contribution is £4,000 and total pension fund investment, including the taxman's top-up, is:

$$£4,000/0.80 = £5,000$$

The £4,000 is what's known as the 'net contribution' and the £5,000 is what's known as the 'gross contribution'.

Multiplying the gross contribution by 20% we get:

$$£5,000 \times 20\% = £1,000$$

This is Peter's additional higher-rate tax relief.

Effectively he has a pension investment of £5,000 which has cost him just £3,000 (£4,000 personal contribution less his £1,000 tax refund). In other words, he is getting all of his investments at a 40% discount.

This is the critical number. Being able to make investments year after year at a 40% discount can have a huge effect on the amount of wealth you accumulate.

Scottish Taxpayers

The Scottish Parliament now has complete power to set income tax rates and thresholds for most types of income, most notably salaries, self-employment income, rental income and pensions. Interest and dividend income are still taxed using UK tax rates and thresholds.

So far there have been no changes to the basic rate, higher rate and additional rate in Scotland. This means Scottish pension savers currently enjoy tax relief at the same rates as pension savers in the rest of the UK.

The one difference is that the higher-rate threshold has been kept at £43,000 for the current 2017/18 tax year. This means Scottish taxpayers can enjoy higher-rate tax relief on their pension contributions once their income exceeds £43,000 (see Chapter 3).

Summary

- When you make pension contributions you qualify for two types of tax relief: Basic-rate tax relief which comes in the shape of top-ups to your pension plan and higher-rate relief which is normally claimed when you submit your tax return.

- Your total pension fund investment is found by dividing your personal contribution by 0.80. The taxman's top-up is paid directly to your pension provider who will credit your pension pot.

- Higher-rate relief is calculated by multiplying your gross pension fund contribution by 20%.

- Together these two tax reliefs mean all your pension investments come in at a 40% discount.

Chapter 2

How Much Can You Invest?

In this chapter we will examine the rules that determine how much you can invest in a pension each year.

Note that successive governments have continually tampered with the pension system, for better or worse. If you are making pension contributions over several decades you should not rely on the same set of rules applying in 5, 10 or 20 years' time.

The good news, for now at least, is that it's possible for most individuals to make quite big pension contributions and enjoy full income tax relief.

Age

This is a good one to kick off with. Generally anyone up to the ripe old age of 75 can make pension contributions.

In the March 2014 Budget the Government announced that it would explore whether this age limit should be changed or abolished. Following consultation, it was decided not to make any changes, so the age limit remains at 75.

There is effectively no lower age limit. You may not be able to set up your own pension plan if you're under 18 years of age but some pension providers have special products so that parents and grandparents can make pension contributions for their children and grandchildren (see Chapter 37 for more information).

Multiple Pension Schemes

Up until a few years ago many members of workplace schemes could not contribute to a second pension, such as a self-invested personal pension (SIPP). This is no longer the case.

Most people can now contribute to more than one pension and have more control over how their retirement savings are invested.

The Basic Pension Contribution Rule

To obtain tax relief on your pension contributions they have to stay within certain limits:

- **Earnings**. Contributions made by you *personally* must not exceed your annual earnings.

- **The £40,000 Annual Allowance.** Total pension contributions by you and anyone else (normally your employer) must not exceed £40,000 per year. The annual allowance is reduced once you start withdrawing certain types of income from your pension (see below). It's also reduced if your "adjusted income" exceeds £150,000 (see Chapter 19 for more details).

Ignoring any pension contributions by the employer, an individual with earnings of £35,000 can contribute £35,000 to a pension. An individual with earnings of £75,000 can contribute £40,000 (contributions capped by the annual allowance).

Employer contributions also have to be thrown into the mix when calculating the maximum pension contribution.

Let's say the individual with earnings of £75,000 is an employee and his employer contributes £10,000 to his pension. The maximum contribution he can make personally is £30,000:

£40,000 annual allowance – £10,000 from employer = £30,000

How Relevant Is this to Me?

Almost everyone making pension contributions needs to understand what is meant by the term 'earnings'. Earnings are not the same as income.

The annual allowance, on the other hand, does not affect most people because most of us do not have anything close to £40,000 paid into our pension plans each year. However, as we shall see in Part 4, there may be times when you want to make big catch-up contributions. In these circumstances it is important to know a bit more about how the annual allowance operates.

Gross vs Cash Contributions

The above pension contribution limits are for *gross* pension contributions. However, the money you actually pay into your pension is normally NOT a gross pension contribution (unless you belong to certain types of occupational pension scheme). To calculate your gross contributions you have to add on basic-rate tax relief (the taxman's top up). You do that by dividing your actual cash contribution by 0.80.

How does this affect the pension contribution limits? If you have earnings of £35,000 you cannot pay £35,000 into your pension plan. You can only pay in £28,000 (£35,000 x 0.8). The taxman will add a further £7,000 in tax relief, bringing your total gross pension contribution to £35,000.

Similarly, the £40,000 annual allowance is a cap on total gross pension contributions. So the maximum cash pension contribution an individual can make in the absence of any employer contributions is £32,000 (£40,000 x 0.8), with the taxman adding a further £8,000 in tax relief.

Employer Contributions

Contributions by employers are always gross contributions. When your employer puts money into your pension plan there is no additional top up from the taxman. Instead the company obtains tax relief by claiming employee pension contributions as a tax deductible business expense.

So if your employer contributes £10,000 to your pension that will be a gross contribution and the maximum gross contribution you can make personally is £30,000:

$$£40,000 - £10,000 = £30,000$$

The maximum amount you can actually pay into your pension plan would then be £24,000:

$$£30,000 \times 0.8 = £24,000$$

You can only make this maximum contribution if you have earnings of at least £30,000.

Occupational Pension Schemes

For many employees who belong to occupational schemes, the actual pension contribution is the same as the gross pension contribution.

Under the popular 'net pay arrangement' the employer often deducts the employee's pension contributions from the employee's gross pay before tax is deducted.

This means full tax relief is obtained immediately by paying the contribution out of pre-tax income. There is no top up by the taxman and no need to claim any higher-rate tax relief via a tax return.

Not all contributions by employees are made gross. If the employer has a pension scheme that uses 'relief at source' (usually group personal pensions), the employee's contributions are paid into the pension scheme after the employee's salary has been taxed. Basic-rate relief is then claimed by the pension scheme and added to the member's pension pot to obtain their total gross pension contribution.

Earnings

To obtain tax relief on your pension contributions you have to have earnings – 'relevant UK earnings' to be precise.

Employees

If you are an employee, your relevant UK earnings will include:

- Salary or wages
- Bonus, overtime, and commissions, and
- Taxable benefits in kind.

There are a few other bits and bobs that can count as relevant UK earnings for pension contribution purposes, including redundancy payments that exceed the £30,000 tax-free threshold and statutory sick pay and statutory maternity pay.

Company Directors

Most small company owners are also directors. For pension contribution purposes company directors are treated just like regular employees. Their relevant UK earnings include their salary, bonus, overtime, commissions and taxable benefits in kind.

As shareholders of their companies they can also pay themselves dividends. To save tax and national insurance, many company owners take a small tax-free salary and take the rest of their income as dividends.

It is often tax efficient for company owners to pay themselves a salary equal to the national insurance threshold (£8,164 for 2017/18) and take the rest of their income as dividends (see Chapter 30).

The problem, however, is that dividends are NOT earnings. As such, a company director with a salary of £8,164 and dividends of £50,000 can only contribute £8,164 to a pension.

The actual cash contribution would be £6,531 (£8,164 x 0.8) with the taxman adding £1,633 in tax relief for a gross contribution of £8,164.

Fortunately for company owners, they can get their companies to make pension contributions (employer contributions) and these are not restricted to their earnings (although they are restricted by the £40,000 annual allowance). We'll take a closer look at pension planning for company owners in Part 7.

The Self-Employed

Most people would regard any business owner as 'self-employed'. However, when HMRC talks about 'self-employed' individuals they are referring specifically to owners of unincorporated businesses, in other words businesses that are not companies.

The most common are sole traders (one-person businesses) and partnerships.

If you are a sole trader your relevant UK earnings are generally the pre-tax profits of the business. If you are a partner, your relevant UK earnings will be your share of the partnership's pre-tax profit.

The problem is that many self-employed individuals don't know what their pre-tax profits are!

Many have an accounting period that is the same as the tax year, running to 5 April each year or 31 March. This can create a practical problem when it comes to maximising tax relief on pension contributions.

Although most salary earners (including company directors) have earnings that are fairly predictable (their salaries), the exact profits on which self-employed business owners can base their pension contributions may not be known until the accounts are drawn up *after* the tax year has ended.

In other words, as a self-employed business owner you may only know what your relevant UK earnings are when it is too late to make pension contributions. You cannot make back-dated pension contributions after the tax year has ended. I'll explain how this practical problem can be fixed in Chapter 33.

Income but Not Earnings

Earnings do not include:

- Rental income
- Interest
- Dividends
- Capital gains

For example, if you have earnings of £30,000 and rental income of £20,000 from buy-to-let properties, the maximum gross pension contribution you can make is £30,000.

With regards to rental income, there is one exception. When it comes to tax, owners of furnished holiday lettings are treated quite differently to other rental property owners and pensions are no exception. Profits from furnished holiday lettings count as relevant UK earnings for pension purposes.

Individuals with No Earnings

Some people don't have any earnings, including non-working spouses and minor children. Many professional landlords, who derive all of their income from rental properties, will also not have any earnings.

The good news is that everyone under the age of 75 can make a pension contribution of £3,600 per year, regardless of earnings. The actual cash contribution would be £2,880, with the taxman adding £720 to bring the total gross contribution to £3,600.

We'll take a closer look at the pros and cons of making pension contributions when you have no earnings in Part 9.

The Annual Allowance

The annual allowance is the overall cap on the amount of pension contributions that enjoy tax relief. It's currently £40,000.

The annual allowance is reduced once you start withdrawing certain types of income from your pension (see below).

The annual allowance is also reduced if your "adjusted income" exceeds £150,000 (see Chapter 19 for more details).

The annual allowance includes pension contributions made by both you and anyone else (normally your employer).

If your contributions do exceed the annual allowance, you can carry forward unused allowance from the three previous years.

If the annual allowance is exceeded, and the excess is not covered by carry forward, the excess is taxed at your marginal income tax rate (20%, 40% or 45%). This annual allowance charge can be paid when you submit your tax return or deducted from your pension savings if it's over £2,000.

In practice, the contribution limits are quite generous and very few people will be affected by them. Those who have to be most careful are those making big one-off pension contributions.

Another group that has to be careful are members of final salary or defined benefit pension schemes. The value of their pension benefits can increase by significantly more than £40,000 in the year they receive a substantial pay increase. Professional advice should also be obtained in these circumstances.

Pension Input Periods

Up until recently, when calculating whether the annual allowance was exceeded, you didn't count pension contributions made during a *tax year* (5 April to 6 April). Instead you used the pension scheme's annual *pension input period*.

As a result, quite big pension contributions made during two different tax years could have fallen into just one pension input period and exceeded the annual allowance.

However, with effect from 6 April 2016 all pension input periods are now aligned with the tax year.

The Carry Forward Rule

If you want to make a big pension contribution that exceeds the annual allowance you can tap any unused allowance from the three previous years.

This means that someone who hasn't made any pension contributions so far during the current tax year can potentially make a pension contribution of up to £160,000 in 2017/18 and enjoy full tax relief:

- £40,000 for 2017/18
- £40,000 for 2016/17
- £40,000 for 2015/16
- £40,000 for 2014/15

Note, the 2015/16 tax year is a bit of an oddity. To allow pension input periods to be aligned with the tax year it had to be split into two "mini tax years": the first starting on 6 April 2015 and ending on 8 July 2015 (mini tax year 1), the second starting on 9 July 2015 and ending on 5 April 2016 (mini tax year 2).

The annual allowance for mini tax year 1 was increased to £80,000. Any of this allowance which wasn't used could be carried forward to mini tax year 2, capped at a maximum of £40,000.

For the purposes of carrying forward unused annual allowance, it is only the unused annual allowance from mini tax year 2 that can be carried forward.

Example
Paula is a sole trader and makes bumper profits of £150,000 during the 2017/18 tax year. She transfers £80,000 into her pension plan, resulting in a gross pension contribution of £100,000 (£80,000/0.8). Her gross pension contributions in the three previous tax years were:

	Pension Contribution	Unused Annual Allowance
2016/17	£20,000	£20,000
2015/16*	£20,000	£20,000
2014/15	£10,000	£30,000

* All contributions made between 9 July 2015 and 5 April 2016.

In total Paula has £70,000 of unused annual allowance. Together with the £40,000 annual allowance for the current tax year, Paula can make a total gross pension contribution of up to £110,000. Her £100,000 gross pension contribution is therefore within the limits and does not exceed her earnings and therefore enjoys full tax relief.

You use the annual allowance for the current tax year first. You then use your unused annual allowance from the *earliest* tax year first (2014/15 in Paula's case).

This leaves any unused allowance from the most recent tax years free to be carried forward. In Paula's case she will be able to carry forward £10,000 of unused allowance from 2016/17 and use it in a future tax year.

Earnings Can't Be Carried Forward

The pension contributions you make personally cannot exceed your earnings for the current tax year. Although you can carry forward unused annual allowance, you cannot carry forward earnings from previous years or make backdated pension contributions.

Membership of a Pension Scheme Required

Unused annual allowance can only be carried forward if you were a member of a registered pension scheme for the period in question.

For example, if you start contributing to a pension now but did not belong to any pension scheme in the three previous tax years, you cannot carry forward any unused annual allowance from those years.

On a practical level, this means that someone who does not currently have a pension plan in place, but may wish to make big contributions in a few years' time, should consider setting one up as soon as possible.

Getting your Contribution Right

The pension contribution rules are quite complex... but only if you have big contributions and are in danger of exceeding the annual allowance.

Most people will not have anything close to £40,000 per year added to their pension pots and are completely unaffected by the annual allowance rules (individuals who want to make big catch-up contributions are an important exception – see Chapter 17).

The earnings limit is also irrelevant for the vast majority of people. Most would never contemplate contributing anything close to 100% of their earnings to a pension. (Company directors are one exception because they often pay themselves a small tax-free salary and therefore have very low 'earnings'.)

I don't want to sound flippant but it's important not to become bogged down by rules that may never affect you. Calculating the maximum pension contribution you *can* make is not the important issue for most people. What is far more important is calculating the maximum pension contribution you *should* make.

A far more important calculation for many individuals is the maximum contribution that will obtain full higher-rate tax relief. This is the subject of the next chapter.

Contributions after Withdrawals Have Started

When you start withdrawing income from your pension your ability to make further pension contributions could be severely restricted.

You may no longer be entitled to a £40,000 annual allowance. Instead your contributions could be restricted by the 'money purchase annual allowance'.

The money purchase annual allowance was due to fall from £10,000 to just £4,000 on 6 April 2017. However, the change was dropped from the 2017 Finance Act, which was rushed through ahead of the June general election.

This measure is still expected to be passed into law. However, at the time of writing it was not known with certainty whether the change would be backdated to 6 April 2017.

There are other anti-avoidance rules designed to prevent money being taken out of a pension in order to make new pension contributions, thereby benefiting from two rounds of tax relief.

If you use your tax-free lump sum to significantly increase your pension contributions, the contributions may fall foul of HMRC's recycling rules and a tax charge of up to 70% could be imposed.

We'll take a closer look at both these issues in Part 2 which deals with taking money out of pensions.

Lifetime Allowance

The lifetime allowance is the maximum amount of money you are allowed to save up in pensions.

It has been steadily reduced in recent years, most recently from £1.25 million to £1 million at the start of the 2016/17 tax year.

Hopefully this was the last cut because, from April 2018, the lifetime allowance will rise each year in line with CPI inflation.

It's impossible to predict what will happen to inflation but if it averages 2% per year, by 2029 the lifetime allowance will be back up to around £1.25 million.

However, there's nothing to stop the current or any future government reversing course and reducing it again!

If you exceed the lifetime allowance you have to pay a lifetime allowance charge, which is 55% if you withdraw the excess funds as a lump sum (before age 75) and 25% if the excess funds are taken out as taxable income.

If you're a basic-rate taxpayer you're usually better off withdrawing the excess funds as taxable income. If you're a higher-rate taxpayer you'll pay roughly the same amount of tax whether you withdraw the excess funds as income or as a lump sum.

How is the Lifetime Allowance Applied?

Your pension pot will be tested against the lifetime allowance when there is a "benefit crystallisation event", typically when you start withdrawing money, including your tax-free lump sum.

The lifetime allowance test also applies if you die before age 75 without having taken any pension benefits or if you reach age 75 with pension savings that haven't been tapped yet.

If you place your pension savings into drawdown when you retire you may face a second lifetime allowance test when you reach age 75 or if use your drawdown funds to buy an annuity.

This second test may affect you if your drawdown fund has grown in size, for example if you've continued working and haven't withdrawn any money from it or have enjoyed superlative investment returns.

But if your drawdown fund has fallen in value (for example, if you've been withdrawing money steadily) there will be nothing additional to measure against the lifetime allowance.

Example

Saul is 65 and has a pension fund worth £800,000. In 2017/18 he takes a tax-free lump sum of £200,000 and moves the remaining £600,000 into drawdown. The lifetime allowance is £1 million in 2017/18 so Saul does not have to pay the lifetime allowance charge. With an £800,000 pension pot this benefit crystallisation event uses up 80% of his lifetime allowance, leaving him with 20% for future use.

He keeps working and doesn't withdraw any income from his drawdown fund. 10 years later his drawdown fund has grown from £600,000 to £1 million. Because he's now 75 there's a second lifetime allowance test. The amount crystallised is the current value of his drawdown fund less its original value: £1 million - £600,000 = £400,000.

Let's assume that when Saul is 75 the lifetime allowance has increased with inflation to £1.2 million. Saul is entitled to 20% of this, i.e. £240,000. Thus Saul will face a lifetime allowance charge on £160,000 (£400,000 - £240,000). The excess funds are subject to a lifetime allowance charge of 25% (£40,000) and he withdraws the rest as taxable income.

It should be fairly easy for Saul to avoid the lifetime allowance charge altogether by simply withdrawing enough money before he is 75. He should withdraw the amount his drawdown fund has grown over and above his remaining lifetime allowance.

Because the withdrawals will be subject to income tax he may be better off doing this over several tax years to avoid paying tax at 40% or more.

Am I in Danger of Exceeding the Lifetime Allowance?

Those most at risk arguably are long-serving members of final salary pension schemes. The annual pension you receive is generally multiplied by 20 and added to any additional lump sum you receive.

For example, with a lifetime allowance of £1 million, someone retiring with a final salary pension of more than £50,000 per year (with no separate lump sum) could be subject to the lifetime allowance charge (£50,000 x 20 = £1 million).

It's also possible that members of money purchase pension schemes (e.g. SIPPs and personal pensions) will breach the limit if they've saved hard or made successful investments.

For example, let's assume future governments do in fact increase the lifetime allowance in line with inflation and inflation averages around 2% per year. In 20 years' time the lifetime allowance will be around £1.5 million and in 30 years' time it will be around £1.8 million.

So if you're 35 and currently have more than around £100,000 of pension savings, growing at around 10% per year, you could breach the lifetime allowance by the time you are 65, *even if you don't make any more pension contributions.*

Similarly, if you're 45 you could exceed the lifetime allowance by the time you're 65 if you currently have more than around £220,000 of pension savings.

Of course, the problem with doing calculations like these over long periods of time is that the outcome can be altered dramatically by tweaking the numbers just slightly.

For example, if we assume that the two individuals' investments grow by 7% per year, instead of 10%, the 35 year old may only exceed the lifetime allowance at age 65 if he has a pension pot of around £240,000 at present. The 45 year old may only exceed the lifetime allowance at age 65 if he has a pension pot of around £385,000 at present. Again this assumes they make no more pension contributions.

What about those who have relatively small pension pots but intend to make regular contributions from now until retirement? Even they could breach the lifetime allowance in some cases.

For example, let's say you're 35 and have not accumulated a single penny of pension savings yet. If you save around £500 per month (and increase the amount you save with inflation) and your investments grow by just over 10% per year, your pension savings could exceed the lifetime allowance by the time you're 65.

Similarly, if you're 45, currently have around £120,000 of pension savings and save £500 per month, you could exceed the lifetime allowance by the time you're 65.

Again, the numbers are sensitive to tweaking and both individuals will fall under the lifetime allowance if their investments grow by just 7% per year.

Remember, in all of the above examples I have assumed that future governments honour the current promise to increase the lifetime allowance in line with inflation. If they don't, then in all of the above examples the individuals will breach the lifetime allowance several years earlier.

However, those who are in danger of exceeding the lifetime allowance may be able to avoid it by simply reducing the amount they save in pensions or taking benefits early.

In summary, those most at risk of breaching the lifetime allowance are long-serving members of final salary pension schemes, those who have already accumulated a reasonable amount of pension savings but are still many years away from retirement, and those who plan to make pension contributions for many years and enjoy above average investment returns.

Protecting Your Lifetime Allowance

If you think you may have more than £1 million of pension savings by the time you retire or reach age 75 you may wish to register for "protection".

There are two new types of protection:

- Fixed protection 2016
- Individual protection 2016

Fixed protection 2016 fixes your lifetime allowance at £1.25 million. To qualify you and your employer must not have made any pension contributions after 5 April 2016 (or have accrued benefits in a final salary scheme).

For individual protection 2016 the value of your pension savings must be more than £1 million on 5 April 2016.

It fixes your lifetime allowance at the lower of £1.25 million or the value of your pensions on 5 April 2016.

It is possible to make further pension contributions after that date.

You can apply online for both types of protection:

www.gov.uk/guidance/pension-schemes-protect-your-lifetime-allowance

There is no deadline to apply for either type of protection, although you must apply before you withdraw money from your pension.

Final Words on the Lifetime Allowance

The lifetime allowance receives a lot of press coverage and for those affected its importance cannot be overstated. However, the reality is that most people are in danger of saving *too little* in pensions, not too much.

Throughout this guide I therefore assume that the reader is not in any danger of breaching the lifetime allowance. If you think you may be affected, it is essential to speak to a professional advisor about your options.

Chapter 3

How to Maximise Your Higher-Rate Tax Relief

Everyone who makes pension contributions gets basic-rate tax relief (the taxman's 20% top up). If you are a higher-rate taxpayer you can also claim an additional 20% tax relief.

However, some higher-rate taxpayers don't enjoy full tax relief on their pension contributions because they don't understand how higher-rate relief is calculated.

It's a bit like paying for a business class ticket and accidentally sitting in economy.

What is a Higher-Rate Taxpayer?

A higher-rate taxpayer is currently someone who has taxable income of more than £45,000 (£43,000 in Scotland – see below).

How is this number calculated? For most individuals the first £11,500 of income is tax free (this is your income tax personal allowance). The next £33,500 is taxed at 20% (your basic-rate band). Once your income rises above £45,000 it's taxed at 40%.

These thresholds are usually changed each year. These are the figures for the 2017/18 tax year.

How Is Higher-Rate Relief Calculated?

When you make pension contributions the taxman gives you a bigger basic-rate band, which means more of your income is taxed at 20% instead of 40%.

Your basic-rate band is increased by the same amount as your *gross* pension contributions.

Example

Sandy is a sole trader with pre-tax profits of £52,000. He has £7,000 of income taxed at 40% (£52,000 - £45,000).

He puts £5,000 into a pension. The taxman adds £1,250 of basic-rate relief for a gross contribution of £6,250 (£5,000/0.8).

To calculate his higher-rate relief his basic-rate band is increased by £6,250, allowing £6,250 of income to be taxed at 20% instead of 40%. This saves Sandy £1,250 in tax (£6,250 x 20%).

This is the best possible outcome. Sandy has received basic-rate and higher-rate tax relief on his entire pension contribution. In total he enjoys 40% tax relief:

$$(£1,250 + £1,250) / £6,250 = 40\%$$

The Maximum Higher Rate Relief

The maximum higher-rate tax relief you can claim is:

Your Gross Pension Contribution x 20%

However, you will only enjoy the maximum higher-rate tax relief if you have at least this much income taxed at 40%.

If your income is £45,000 plus one pound, you can only get higher-rate tax relief on one pound of pension contributions.

Sandy, whose income is £52,000, can get higher-rate tax relief on a gross pension contribution of up to £7,000 (£52,000 – £45,000). His actual gross pension contribution is £6,250 so he has stayed within the limits. If he contributes more than £7,000, the additional contribution will only get basic-rate relief.

Tax Planning

Big pension contributions can be a bad idea if you don't have enough income taxed at 40%.

To enjoy the maximum tax relief you may want to consider spreading your pension contributions over a number of tax years.

If maximising tax relief is your priority, you should make sure your gross pension contributions do not exceed the amount of income you have taxed at 40%.

Example revisited

Sandy is a sole trader with pre-tax profits of £52,000 in 2017/18. He has £7,000 of income taxed at 40% (£52,000 - £45,000).

Sandy puts £15,000 into his pension. The taxman adds £3,750 of basic-rate relief. His gross contribution is £18,750 (£15,000/0.8).

His basic-rate band is increased by £18,750 which means his maximum higher-rate tax relief is:

$$£18,750 \times 20\% = £3,750$$

However, Sandy doesn't have £18,750 of income taxed at 40%, he only has £7,000. So the actual higher-rate relief he will receive is:

$$£7,000 \times 20\% = £1,400$$

Although his basic-rate band has been increased significantly, he doesn't have enough income to use it! Sandy is only obtaining higher-rate tax relief on £7,000 worth of pension contributions. In total he enjoys just 27% tax relief:

$$(£3,750 + £1,400) / £18,750 = 27\%$$

What can Sandy do if he wants to enjoy the maximum higher-rate relief? He can spread his contributions over several tax years.

If he wants to invest £15,000 (£18,750 gross) and if we assume he has £7,000 of income per year taxed at 40%, this means he could consider spreading his gross contributions over three tax years:

Year 1	£7,000
Year 2	£7,000
Year 3	£4,750

Table 1
Maximising Higher-Rate Tax Relief:
Maximum Pension Contributions 2017/18

Taxable Income £	Maximum Gross Contribution £	Maximum Net Contribution £
45,000	0	0
50,000	5,000	4,000
55,000	10,000	8,000
60,000	15,000	12,000
65,000	20,000	16,000
70,000	25,000	20,000
75,000	30,000	24,000
80,000	35,000	28,000
85,000	40,000	32,000
90,000	45,000	36,000
95,000	50,000	40,000
100,000	55,000	44,000

Rule of Thumb

If maximising tax relief is your priority, the maximum amount you should contribute to a pension in the 2017/18 tax year is:

Your taxable income <u>minus</u> *£45,000*

This is your maximum *gross* pension contribution. Multiply this number by 0.8 to obtain the maximum amount you can actually invest (your net cash contribution).

Table 1 contains some sample maximum pension contributions for different levels of income.

Although you can contribute up to £40,000 per year to a pension (ignoring any employer contributions), only someone with income of at least £85,000 would enjoy full higher-rate tax relief on such a large gross contribution:

£85,000 - £45,000 = £40,000

Someone with income over £85,000 could contribute more than £40,000 and enjoy higher-rate tax relief on the entire contribution. However, to do this in practice they would have to carry forward unused annual allowance from previous tax years.

Big Contributions Close to Retirement

When you are close to retirement it may be worth making pension contributions that are larger than normal, even if you only enjoy basic-rate tax relief.

This is because it is possible to withdraw all the extra money you contribute immediately after you retire and 25% will be tax free.

We'll take a look at the potential tax savings in Chapter 10.

Taxpayers with Dividend Income

Some taxpayers whose *non-dividend* income is close to the higher-rate threshold may not enjoy full higher-rate relief on their pension contributions if they also have dividend income.

Example
In 2017/18 Alistair has salary and rental income of £50,000. The final £5,000 of this income is subject to higher-rate tax. He also has dividend income of £10,000. The first £5,000 is tax free thanks to the dividend allowance. The final £5,000 is taxed at 32.5%. (See Chapter 30 for more information about how dividends are taxed.)

If Alistair makes a gross pension contribution of £10,000 his basic-rate band will be increased by £10,000. This means the final £5,000 of his salary and rental income will be taxed at 20% instead of 40%, saving him £1,000.

The first £5,000 of his dividends will also fall into his increased basic-rate band BUT this income is tax free anyway, thanks to the £5,000 dividend allowance. So there is no higher-rate tax relief on this income.

If instead Alistair had salary and rental income of £55,000, he would enjoy the full £2,000 of higher-rate tax relief on his pension contribution: Instead of paying 40% tax on the final £10,000 of this income, he would pay just 20% tax.

This example may only be relevant to a small number of taxpayers. Nevertheless, what it reveals is you will not enjoy full higher-rate tax relief on your pension contributions if the first £5,000 of your dividend income falls into your increased basic-rate band.

Note the dividend allowance is expected to fall from £5,000 to £2,000 in April 2018.

Higher-Rate Taxpayers in Scotland

In Scotland the higher-rate threshold for the current 2017/18 tax year has been frozen at £43,000. So if you're a Scottish taxpayer, the maximum amount you should contribute to a pension if you want full higher-rate relief is:

Your taxable income minus *£43,000*

For example, a Scottish taxpayer who earns £50,000 can make a gross pension contribution of £7,000 which means a net cash contribution of £5,600.

Remember the Scottish Parliament can tax most types of income but NOT interest and dividends. So if you are a company owner in Scotland and pay yourself a small salary and the rest of your income comes in the shape of dividends, the relevant higher-rate threshold is the "Westminster" one – £45,000. (See Chapter 30 for more on how company directors structure their pay.)

Example
Angus is a sole trader based in Scotland with taxable income of £45,000 in 2017/18. Angus can make a gross pension contribution of £2,000 with full higher-rate tax relief.

Douglas is a company owner based in Scotland with the same amount of taxable income (£45,000) but made up mostly of dividend income.

If Douglas makes a pension contribution of £2,000 he will not enjoy any higher-rate tax relief because he is not a higher-rate taxpayer (the UK, not Scottish, higher-rate threshold applies to his dividend income).

Chapter 4

How to Claim Higher-Rate Tax Relief

Approximately 200,000 higher-rate taxpayers do not claim their higher-rate tax relief, losing roughly £1,300 per year each on average.

Many taxpayers believe incorrectly that all of their pension tax relief is automatically credited to their pension pots.

Those who usually do NOT have to claim higher-rate tax relief are members of occupational money purchase pension schemes. Their pension contributions are paid out of their salaries before tax is deducted, so full 40% tax relief is effectively granted immediately.

Those who are affected include members of group personal pensions, group stakeholder pensions and group SIPPs. With these arrangements the contributions are made out of after-tax pay, so tax relief has to be actively claimed.

Individuals with their own private pension plans also have to actively claim their higher-rate tax relief.

Gross vs Net Contributions

Another mistake made by higher-rate taxpayers when completing tax returns is entering net cash pension contributions (the amount they actually pay in), instead of their gross contributions (which include the taxman's basic-rate tax relief top up).

Page 4 of your tax return is for 'Tax reliefs'. Box 1 asks for:

Payments to registered pension schemes where basic rate tax relief will be claimed by your pension provider (called 'relief at source'). Enter the payments and basic rate tax

If you personally pay £3,000 into your pension and insert this number on your tax return, the taxman will give you £600 of higher-rate tax relief:

$$£3,000 \times 20\% = £600$$

But if you enter the correct amount, which is £3,750 (£3,000/0.8), the taxman will give you £750 of higher-rate tax relief:

$$£3,750 \times 20\% = £750$$

Do not include employer pension contributions.

Backdated Claims

If you have not claimed your higher-rate tax relief, the good news is you can make a backdated claim going back four years. Rebates can run to thousands of pounds.

Write to your local tax office, outlining the gross contributions you have made and the tax years they relate to, or speak to an accountant.

How to Claim Higher-Rate Tax Relief

The standard way to claim higher-rate tax relief is when you submit your tax return. You can also claim it through an adjustment to your tax code. This allows tax relief to be provided immediately because less tax will be deducted from your salary each month.

(A tax code is used by your employer to calculate the amount of tax to deduct from your pay. If you have the wrong tax code you could end up paying too much tax.)

You can have your tax code adjusted by contacting HMRC and some pension companies provide template letters for this purpose.

You may need to contact HMRC again if your pension contributions increase, for example if you get a pay increase or if you make one-off contributions during the year.

Chapter 5

Higher-Rate Tax Relief: Here to Stay?

"The gross cost of pensions tax relief is significant. Including relief on both income tax and national insurance contributions, the government forwent nearly £50 billion in 2013-14." HM Treasury

For several years now there have been fears the Government will take away the additional tax relief enjoyed by higher-rate taxpayers on their pension contributions.

Up until now this has been done *indirectly* by reducing the annual allowance (the amount that can be paid into a pension each year) from £255,000 to £40,000.

A further clamp down on high income earners came into effect on 6 April 2016. The £40,000 annual allowance is reduced if your 'adjusted income' is more than £150,000. (See Chapter 19 for more details.)

Pensions – More Changes Ahead?

David Cameron's government consulted on whether it would be a good idea to completely reform pension tax relief and an announcement was expected in the March 2016 Budget.

However, in that Budget speech Chancellor George Osborne stated that "it was clear there is no consensus" and pension tax relief was left unchanged.

Apparently the decision not to reduce tax relief on pension contributions was made so as not to antagonize voters ahead of the EU referendum!

What about the new Conservative Government?

Following the March 2017 Budget there were reports in some newspapers that Chancellor Philip Hammond had made cutting pension tax relief a priority, following his embarrassing u-turn over national insurance for the self-employed, which left a hole in the public finances.

However, there was no mention of cutting pension tax relief in the Conservatives' 2017 election manifesto, so it is unclear whether there will be a further tax raid on pensions or if taxes will be raised by other means. The Conservatives have ditched their previous commitment to not raise income tax and national insurance rates.

If there is a further raid on pension tax relief it could take the shape of a further reduction in the annual allowance (from, say, £40,000 to £30,000) or replacing higher-rate tax relief with a flat-rate model where everyone gets tax relief at, say, 25% or 30%, regardless of income.

The truth is nobody knows what will happen to pensions in the months and years ahead, although further changes seem likely at some point.

For several years now pension companies have advised higher-rate taxpayers to make bigger pension contributions before their additional tax relief is scrapped. To date all such predictions have been proved wrong.

Nevertheless, many higher-rate taxpayers may feel they have nothing to lose by making hay while the sun is still shining, i.e. making pension contributions with 40% tax relief sooner rather than later.

Part 2

Taking Money Out: The New Pension Freedom Rules

Chapter 6

Introduction

Before Age 55

At present you cannot withdraw any money from your pension until you're 55. This is one of the major drawbacks with pensions. There are times in life when even financially conservative individuals may need to tap their retirement savings early.

Obvious examples would be to pay for a child's education or unforeseen family medical expenses. In the worst case scenario you may even need to access your savings early to avoid bankruptcy or home repossession. So if you're under 55 and want to make significant pension contributions you should make sure you have other resources to protect against:

- Unforeseen expenses, and an
- Unforeseen drop in income.

Although you cannot withdraw anything until you're 55, it's important to point out that the money can usually be invested as you please. These days many personal pensions plans, especially SIPPs, provide enormous investment flexibility.

Note too that 55 is the minimum age set out in the legislation. Some company pension schemes stipulate a later retirement age and you may need permission to start withdrawing money earlier.

The Ill Health Exceptions

There are two exceptions to the no withdrawals before age 55 rule... but if you are squeamish you should look away now. All pension savings can be withdrawn as a lump sum if you suffer from "serious ill health" (the polite way of saying you have less than a year to live). These are tax free before age 75, taxable after age 75. You may also be able to start withdrawing money from your pension if you suffer from "ill health" (which means you are not about to die but are too sick to work again).

Future Changes to the Pension Age

In 2028 the minimum pension age is expected to increase from 55 to 57, when the state pension age increases to 67. So if you were born after April 1973, you will have to wait at least another two years before you can tap your savings.

The minimum age is then expected to increase in line with the state pension age, so that it is always 10 years below state pension age. Thus the minimum age for making pension withdrawals may increase to 58 by the mid 2030s and 59 by the late 2040s.

Proposals to Increase the Pension Age Sooner

It is possible the minimum pension age will be raised even faster. In March 2015 the Works and Pensions Committee published a report which stated that:

"Our view is that, given the significant tax relief provided to pensions, increased longevity, and the importance of ensuring people do not underestimate the income needed in retirement, the minimum age at which people can access their pension saving, except on ill health grounds, should rise to five years below the State Pension age."

Presumably they were recommending raising the minimum age from 55 to 60 as soon as possible. Of course, this proposal may never make it onto the statute books but you certainly can't rule it out now that the genie is out of the bottle. Even if such a change were made many years from now, it would still have the same impact on those who are many years away from retirement.

This brings us neatly to the other major drawback of using pensions: almost every benefit can be taken away by politicians. They can change the age limits and tax reliefs, restrict how you invest your savings and make withdrawals and increase the tax paid on the money you take out or leave to your family.

Recent changes have definitely been for the better; future ones could be for the worse – politicians love to make gifts and then take them back!

Pension Freedom

When you're 55 (or older in future) you can start tapping your pension. You can take out as much money as you like, whenever you like.

You can withdraw the whole lot in one go or leave your entire pension pot untouched and give it to your family when you die (see Chapter 9).

Most people will probably do something in between these two extremes. For example, when you're 55 you could take your tax-free lump sum and leave the rest of your savings to grow tax free until you retire and then start withdrawing income gradually.

Saving tax will be a key consideration (see Chapter 10).

Under the new rules you can use one or more of the following products to access your pension:

- Flexi-access drawdown
- Uncrystallised funds pension lump sum (UFPLS)
- Lifetime annuity

Flexi-access drawdown lets you take your entire tax-free lump sum in one go and place your remaining savings into drawdown, where the money can be accessed as and when you like.

Taking an uncrystallised funds pension lump sum allows you to take your tax-free lump sum in stages instead of in one go. Like drawdown, you can make withdrawals as and when you like but one quarter of every withdrawal will be tax free with the remainder taxed as income.

Annuities have always been on the menu but are extremely unpopular these days because they pay a miniscule amount of income. They're also unpopular because the life insurance company generally confiscates your pension savings when you die or your spouse dies. Despite their drawbacks, annuities do nevertheless provide a guaranteed "risk-free" income for life, unlike drawdown and UFPLS.

The various income options are discussed further in the next chapter.

Final Salary Pensions

The pension freedom reforms apply to "defined contribution" pensions only: personal pensions and SIPPs and many occupational pension schemes in the private sector.

They're not available to members of final salary pension schemes (also known as defined benefit schemes). Members of these schemes cannot withdraw as much money as they like, whenever they like.

However, if you belong to a final salary scheme it may be possible to transfer to a defined contribution scheme (e.g. a SIPP) and collect a large cash lump sum.

This is currently a "hot topic" for members of defined benefit pension schemes because transfer values of around 25 to 40 times the annual pension have been offered in recent times. So someone who expects to receive a pension of, say, £25,000 per year could be offered a lump sum well in excess of £600,000.

Transferring to a personal pension may also allow you to access your pension savings earlier (for example, at age 55 instead of at age 60 or 65) and leave surplus funds to your children.

However, pension transfers are also highly controversial, which is why professional advice is necessary in most cases.

Many pension experts advise against transferring from a "gold-plated" final salary scheme, which offers a guaranteed income for life, to a "crummy" personal pension, where your retirement income will depend on how well your investments perform. Members of final salary schemes do not have to worry about the ups and downs of the stock market!

Members of unfunded public sector pension schemes (i.e. teachers, NHS employees and civil servants) are not able to transfer to a defined contribution scheme and access their pension as a lump sum. Unfunded pension schemes are ones that don't have any assets – they rely on taxpayers to keep up the pension payments.

Members of funded public sector schemes (such as the local government pension scheme) are able to transfer to a defined contribution scheme.

Tax on Pension Withdrawals

Although you can take one quarter of your pension savings as a tax-free lump sum, you have to pay income tax on everything else you withdraw, *including your original contributions*.

That's a bit like putting £100 in a bank account and paying £20 or maybe £40 tax when you withdraw the money a year later. Of course, this doesn't happen when you withdraw money from your bank account – at most you will pay tax on your interest.

So while pensions offer several tax concessions, there is a tax sting at the end.

Thus, the sixty-four-thousand dollar question is this:

Do the tax benefits – tax relief on contributions and tax-free investment growth – outweigh the penalty of heavily taxed withdrawals?

In most cases the answer is "Yes". This is because most people will probably pay no more than 20% tax on the money they take out but will enjoy 40% tax relief when they put their money in, if they are higher-rate taxpayers.

Furthermore, some of the money you take out will be tax free, including your tax-free lump sum and any withdrawals that are covered by your income tax personal allowance.

This is why even basic-rate taxpayers will usually also end up better off with a pension. Although they only enjoy 20% tax relief when they put their money in, a significant chunk of the money they take out will be tax free.

But *exactly* how much better off are you likely to be with a pension? The benefits surely have to be significant to justify putting your money into a locked box until you're 55 or older.

One way to answer this question is to compare two investors: one putting money into a pension and the other putting money into a different tax shelter, an ISA, and see who ends up better off at the end of the day.

We do this in Chapter 14.

Like pensions, money in ISAs grows tax free. However, unlike pensions, ISAs do not offer any upfront tax relief but all your withdrawals are tax free and your money is not tied up until age 55 or later – you can withdraw it whenever you like.

However, the problem with using ISAs as retirement saving vehicles is they give you tax relief when you may need it least.

It's usually better to have 40% tax relief when you put your money in, as you do with pensions if you're a higher-rate taxpayer, rather than 20% tax relief when you take it out, as you would with ISAs (most individuals only pay 20% tax when they retire).

If you're under 40 you can now also invest in a Lifetime ISA. These arguably offer the best of both worlds: upfront tax relief (in the shape of a Government bonus) and tax-free withdrawals. We also compare Lifetime ISAs and pensions in Chapter 14.

Pension Advice

From April 2017 a new Pensions Advice Allowance has been introduced. This allows you to withdraw £500 tax free from your pension pot on three occasions (i.e. three separate tax years) to pay for pensions and retirement advice.

The allowance will be available at any age and to members of defined contribution pension schemes (not final salary pension schemes).

Chapter 7

Flexi-Access Drawdown & UFPLS

If you want to make use of the new flexible regime for pension withdrawals you have two choices:

- Flexi-access drawdown
- Uncrystallised funds pension lump sum (UFPLS)

Some pension providers will only offer very limited options so you may have to shop around and, in some cases, it may even be necessary to transfer your pension to another provider.

Flexi-Access Drawdown

When you reach pension age (currently 55) you can move some or all of your pension savings into flexi-access drawdown.

One quarter (25%) can be taken as a tax-free cash lump sum and only flexi-access drawdown allows you to take your tax-free lump sum on its own without any additional taxable income (for example, if you want to withdraw some cash to pay off your mortgage before you stop working).

The remaining 75% continues to grow tax free in your drawdown fund until you withdraw it. You can withdraw as much income as you like whenever you like. All withdrawals will be fully taxed.

If at any point you decide you want a more secure income for the rest of your life, you can use some or all of your remaining drawdown funds to buy an annuity.

Phased Drawdown

If you don't want to take your entire tax-free lump sum in one go, you can use something called phased drawdown. For example, you may wish to withdraw a small tax-free lump sum to reduce your mortgage or for home improvements.

Phased drawdown may also appeal to those who are semi-retired. It allows you to make regular tax-free withdrawals to supplement your income before you are fully retired.

Then when you stop working completely (and your tax rate is hopefully lower) you can start withdrawing money from the taxable portion of your pension pot.

By not withdrawing your entire lump sum in one go it can continue to grow tax free inside your pension. As a result you may end up with more tax-free cash overall.

Example
Stacey is 58 and still working and has a pension pot worth £200,000. She wants to take just £10,000 out of her pension tax free. She transfers £40,000 into a flexi-access drawdown plan and takes the 25% tax-free lump sum of £10,000 and leaves the remaining £30,000 in the drawdown plan without taking any additional taxable income.

A couple of years later she transfers another £40,000 into the drawdown plan and takes another £10,000 of tax-free cash. She leaves the remaining £30,000 in the drawdown plan, along with the other £30,000 from two years ago.

She can keep doing this until she has transferred all of her pension pot into flexi-access drawdown.

Uncrystallised Funds Pension Lump Sum (UFPLS)

The recent pension reforms were clearly made in a hurry. How else can you explain calling something an "uncrystallised funds pension lump sum", with the unwieldy acronym UFPLS?

With UFPLS you can take your entire pension pot as a lump sum in one go, or take a series of smaller lump sums. Each lump sum will have a 25% tax-free element, with the rest taxed as income.

UFPLS may appeal to those who don't need all their tax-free cash immediately. Instead it can continue to grow tax free. Note, however, that a similar result can be achieved with flexi-access drawdown by using phased drawdown (if your pension provider offers it) and crystallising just a portion of your retirement savings.

Example
Zach has a £100,000 pension pot. He withdraws £20,000 using UFPLS, leaving £80,000 in his pension pot. £5,000 of the UFPLS is tax-free cash, the remaining £15,000 is taxable. If we assume Zach has other income and is a basic-rate taxpayer he will pay 20% tax: £3,000. Zach can continue to use UFPLS to take lump sums as and when he needs. He can also move his remaining pension pot into flexi-access drawdown or, if he wants a secure income for the rest of his life with no investment risk, he can use his remaining funds to buy an annuity.

With UFPLS you have to take tax-free cash and taxable income at the same time – every withdrawal will consist of 25% tax-free cash and 75% taxable income.

Flexi-access drawdown is therefore more flexible because it lets you take tax-free cash without having to take any taxable income. This may be more appealing if you want to withdraw cash while you are still working and paying 40% tax. You can postpone withdrawing taxable income until you retire and start paying tax at 20% (most retirees are basic-rate taxpayers).

The Money Purchase Annual Allowance (MPAA)

When you start withdrawing money from your pension pot you can continue making pension contributions but you may be subject to the money purchase annual allowance (MPAA).

The money purchase annual allowance is currently £10,000 but is expected to be reduced to £4,000, possibly backdated to 6 April 2017. The position is not entirely clear because the change was dropped from the 2017 Finance Act, which was rushed through ahead of the June general election.

The reduction in the money purchase annual allowance is still expected to be passed into law. However, at the time of writing it was not known with certainty whether the change would apply from 6 April 2017, 6 April 2018 or some other date.

If the change is passed into law it will have a significant impact on some individuals. Being limited to an annual pension contribution of just £4,000 (compared with the normal £40,000 annual allowance) will make it very difficult for those who have accessed their pension savings (perhaps through financial hardship) to rebuild them.

If you are subject to the money purchase annual allowance you also cannot carry forward any unused allowance from previous tax years.

Note that £4,000 would be the maximum *gross* pension contribution you could make. The maximum cash you could invest personally would be £3,200. The taxman would add £800 of basic-rate tax relief to produce a gross pension contribution of £4,000.

If you use flexi-access drawdown and take your 25% tax-free lump but do not withdraw any additional taxable income, you get to keep your £40,000 annual allowance, i.e. you can keep making pension contributions just like anyone else.

However, as soon as you take any income from your drawdown fund the money purchase annual allowance will apply.

With uncrystallised funds pension lump sums (UFPLS) the money purchase annual allowance applies once you start making any pension withdrawals. In other words, as soon as you start withdrawing money using UFPLS your pension contributions could be restricted to £4,000 per year.

Thus, flexi-access drawdown may be more suitable for those who want to keep making pension contributions. You can withdraw some or all of your tax-free cash and keep making pension contributions of up to £40,000 per year and use your unused annual allowance from the previous three tax years.

The money purchase annual allowance was introduced to reduce pension recycling – taking income out of a pension and using it to make fresh contributions with tax relief.

It is also designed to prevent those aged 55 and over replacing their regular taxed salaries with employer pension contributions, 25% of which could be withdrawn tax free immediately.

Note that additional rules prevent tax-free lump sums being recycled (see Chapter 8).

The MPAA only applies to money purchase pension contributions (e.g. those paid into personal pensions and SIPPs). It does not restrict contributions to defined benefit pension schemes (final salary schemes).

In other words, your annual allowance for funding a final salary scheme will generally still be £40,000, less any money purchase contributions within the £4,000 limit.

The money purchase annual allowance also isn't triggered if:

- You use your pension pot to buy a standard lifetime annuity

- You are using capped drawdown (the old type of drawdown that is no longer available to new retirees) and do not withdraw income above the maximum income limit

- You cash in a small pension pot. You can take up to three pension pots worth up to £10,000 each (an unlimited number from occupational pension schemes)

PAYE Issues

When you withdraw income from your pension, the pension provider will deduct tax before paying you.

If your pension provider does not hold a current P45 form for you (usually only issued when you stop working), tax will be deducted at the so-called emergency rate. In many cases this will mean that far too much tax is deducted and you will be due a refund.

For example, if you withdraw £10,000 from your pension at the start of the tax year you could be taxed as if your total income is £120,000 for the year.

The refund can be claimed at the end of the tax year or you can claim the tax back during the year (apparently within 30 days).

If you decide to make a single withdrawal that does not empty your pension pot, you can claim back the tax overpaid by completing a P55 form.

Those intending to make a series of irregular withdrawals are advised to talk to their pension providers. After applying emergency tax to the first payment, the pension provider might be able to report a zero payment for the months where no withdrawal is made and correct the tax deducted on subsequent withdrawals.

Another new form P50Z is to be used if you empty your entire pension pot in a single withdrawal and have no other PAYE or pension income (other than your state pension). Form P53Z should be used if you have other employment income or pensions.

Chapter 8

The Pension Recycling Rules

When you start withdrawing income from a flexi-access drawdown plan or make any withdrawal using UFPLS, you will be subject to the money purchase annual allowance.

This may limit your future money purchase pension contributions to £4,000 per year and prohibit you from carrying forward any unused annual allowance from previous tax years.

If you use flexi-access drawdown and withdraw your tax-free lump sum only (with no additional income) you can continue making pension contributions of up to £40,000 per year (if you have sufficient earnings) and use any unused annual allowance from the previous three tax years.

However, if you use your tax-free lump sum to make new pension contributions, you have to be wary of HMRC's recycling rules. These are designed to prevent tax-free cash being reinvested in a pension and enjoying a second round of tax relief.

Example
Toby is 59, still working and a higher-rate taxpayer. Over the last 10 years he has been making pension contributions of £6,000 per year. Using flexi-access drawdown he withdraws £10,000 of tax-free cash in order to reinvest it in a pension. The taxman adds £2,500 of basic-rate tax relief, giving him a total gross pension contribution of £12,500. Furthermore, when he submits his tax return he receives higher-rate tax relief of £2,500.

Unfortunately for Toby his pension contribution may fall foul of HMRC's recycling rules which are designed to prevent you making larger than normal pension contributions because you have received a tax-free lump sum.

The recycling rules can even apply if you make bigger than normal pension contributions *before* you withdraw tax-free cash.

If the recycling rules apply, your tax-free lump sum will be treated as an unauthorised payment, resulting in a tax charge of up to 70%.

The recycling rules apply when ALL of the following conditions are met:

- You take a tax-free cash lump sum from your pension

- The tax-free cash, including any tax-free cash taken in the previous 12 months, exceeds £7,500

- Because you took tax-free cash your pension contributions are significantly larger than they otherwise would be

- The additional contributions are more than 30% of the tax-free cash

- The recycling was pre-planned

Point 2 means that small amounts of recycling effectively fall under the radar.

Example
Using phased drawdown Justine takes a tax-free lump sum of £7,000 and immediately invests all of it in a pension plan, producing a gross pension contribution of £8,750 after basic-rate tax relief is added. She hasn't received any other tax-free cash in the previous 12 months so the pension contribution does not fall foul of the recycling rules, even though the recycling was pre-planned.

Looking at point 3, for the recycling rules to apply there must be a significant increase in your pension contributions. This includes contributions made by you and your employer.

HMRC will look at your contribution history to determine if there has been a significant increase. If you haven't made any pension contributions for a while, your last contribution may be adjusted for inflation to produce a current value for comparison purposes.

As a rule of thumb, HMRC may argue that your pension contributions have increased significantly if they are 30% larger than they would have been without the tax-free cash.

HMRC doesn't just look for big pension contributions in the tax year you receive tax-free cash. They will also look at contributions made in the two tax years before you received the cash and in the two tax years after you took the cash.

Example
Harvey is 60 and for the last five years has been making pension contributions of £10,000 per year. He takes a £40,000 tax-free lump sum from his pension and uses some of it to pay for a new kitchen and the rest to make a £25,000 pension contribution in the next tax year. Because his pension contribution is more than 30% larger than those made in recent years he may fall foul of the pension recycling rules.

The amount of additional contributions is measured on a cumulative basis which means you may be caught out even if you only make relatively small additional pension contributions after receiving your tax-free cash.

Example
Joan has been making pension contributions of £10,000 per year for the last 10 years. She takes £20,000 of tax-free cash from her pension and uses some of it to increase her pension contributions as follows:

	Contribution	Increase	% Increase
Current year	£12,500	£2,500	25%
One year later	£12,500	£2,500	25%
Two years later	£12,500	£2,500	25%
Cumulative increase		£7,500	75%

Joan's pension contributions have not increased by more than 30% in any single year but the cumulative increase is 75%. This is more than 30% which means there has been a significant increase.

Because the additional pension contributions were pre-planned she may have to pay £14,000 tax on the £20,000 tax-free lump sum.

Turning to point 4, you'll only be caught by the recycling rules if your additional contributions are more than 30% of your tax-free lump sum. In Joan's case her additional contributions were £7,500 and are more than 30% of her tax-free lump sum (£20,000 x 30% = £6,000).

However, if her additional contributions were less than £2,000 per year (less than £6,000 in total) this would presumably not count as pension recycling.

Point 5 is the most vague. The recycling must be pre-planned which means you must have intended to take your tax-free lump sum to make significantly greater pension contributions.

If you decide to use your tax-free lump sum to significantly increase your pension contributions but make the contributions *before* receiving your tax-free lump sum this will also be treated as pre-planning (for example, if you use other savings or a loan to pay the contributions and then use your lump sum to replenish those savings or pay off the loan).

Where, on the other hand, you take a lump sum and only later decide to use it to make bigger contributions, there is no pre-planning.

When the Recycling Rules Do Not Apply

The key is that the recycling rules only apply when your pension contributions are significantly increased "because of" the tax-free lump sum.

There are other reasons why your pension contributions may increase significantly from year to year and they will not constitute recycling.

For example, let's say you increase your pension contributions from £10,000 to £15,000 in the year you take tax-free cash. Although your pension contributions have increased by more than 30% this may be because you've received a bonus or the profits of your business have increased or because you have more income taxed at 40% and want to maximise your higher-rate tax relief.

As long as you can demonstrate that, although your pension contributions have fluctuated, they are calculated on a consistent basis (e.g. as a percentage of your income) the recycling rules should not apply.

The recycling rules will also not apply if you make significantly larger pension contributions because you receive a cash windfall such as an inheritance.

Example
Sadie takes tax-free cash from her pension. A few months later her father dies leaving her a substantial lump sum. Because of the inheritance (and not because she received a pension lump sum), she decides to make larger than normal pension contributions. She invests the whole inheritance in her pension. These pension contributions will not constitute recycling because she did not pre-plan to use the pension lump sum to make significantly larger pension contributions.

In summary, it is probably possible to trickle some of your tax-free lump sum back into a pension, providing the additional annual contributions are very small and made over many tax years.

However, it's important to stress that this is high-risk tax planning because if you get it wrong the penalties are severe.

Anyone thinking of making larger than normal pension contributions a couple of years before or after taking tax-free cash should probably seek professional advice.

Chapter 9

Leaving Your Pension Pot to Your Family

Pensions have become a lot more attractive when it comes to leaving money to your family.

After you die your pension pot can be transferred tax free to any member of your family (or anyone else for that matter).

The new rules apply from 6 April 2015.

Under the old rules, a 55% "death tax" was generally payable, leaving just 45% for your family.

The 55% tax could be avoided by using your pension savings to provide a "dependant's pension" for your spouse or children under 23. Of course, most people die when their children are over 23, so it usually wasn't possible to leave pension savings to children without paying the death tax.

The rules were more generous if you died before age 75 – your entire pension pot could be paid out tax free to your family... *but only if you hadn't started taking out any money.*

The New Rules

Death before Age 75

Your pension savings can be paid tax free to any beneficiary. It doesn't matter whether you've started withdrawing money or not.

Your beneficiaries can take the money as a tax-free lump sum or keep the money invested in a drawdown plan and make tax free withdrawals as and when they like – they don't have to wait until reaching the minimum pension age (currently 55).

The drawdown investments will continue to grow tax free until income is withdrawn.

Lump sum death benefits are only tax free if paid out within two years of the pension scheme administrator becoming aware of the member's death. Similarly, where uncrystallised pension savings are placed into flexi-access drawdown, withdrawals will only be tax-free if the drawdown designation is made within two years.

75 or Older

The 55% death tax has been abolished which means your beneficiaries can inherit all of your pension savings.

They will still have to pay income tax on any money they withdraw, just like you would, but they can also keep the money invested where it will continue to grow tax free for as long as they like, perhaps until they themselves retire.

There are no restrictions on the amount of income they can withdraw, i.e. the whole pension pot can be paid out in a single tax year, although this may not be very tax efficient.

Example
Helen dies aged 80, leaving pension savings of £100,000. Her son Kevin is her nominated beneficiary. He earns a salary of £60,000 per year. Helen's pension savings are placed into a drawdown plan for Kevin and he withdraws all the money as income during the current tax year.

Kevin will end up paying additional tax of £45,100 on the pension withdrawal. This is because his income for the year is now £160,000 which means he loses his income tax personal allowance and pays 45% tax on some of the pension withdrawal.

It may be more tax efficient for Kevin to leave the money growing tax free in the drawdown plan until he himself retires and then start making gradual withdrawals which will probably be taxed at 20%.

Where the pension plan does not offer flexi-access drawdown the pension savings can be paid as a lump sum which will be subject to income tax in the hands of the recipient.

Inheritance Tax

It's important to point out that pensions are typically held in trust outside your estate and are thus free from inheritance tax in most cases.

This is because the administrator of the pension scheme normally has discretion over who gets the money, although they will typically be guided by your wishes, which can be stated by completing a simple expression of wishes form.

Because these forms are usually not legally binding (although rarely ignored), your pension savings will not form part of your estate for IHT purposes.

There are, however, some exceptions to the general "no inheritance tax on pensions" rule:

- Pension contributions made while you are in ill health or within two years of death may still be subject to inheritance tax.

- Certain retirement annuity contracts (not sold after 1988) and section 32 deferred annuity contracts may form part of your estate for inheritance tax purposes.

- Death benefits paid from NEST (the new workplace pension set up by the Government) are potentially subject to inheritance tax.

Tax Planning

With the 55% death tax now abolished, combined with an exemption from inheritance tax in most cases, pensions pots are potentially powerful vehicles for passing wealth tax free from one generation to another.

The assets in the plan will continue to grow tax free and the only tax payable by your beneficiaries will be income tax on withdrawals. They won't pay any income tax on their withdrawals if you die before age 75.

Your nominated beneficiaries (e.g. your children) can then pass on any unused funds to their own nominated beneficiaries (e.g. your grandchildren) and so on.

The grandchildren will pay tax on their withdrawals if your children die after reaching age 75. No tax will be payable if your children die before age 75.

Preserving Your Pension Pot

Because pension pots are potentially useful inheritance tax shelters, some advisers recommend that wealthy retirees who are worried about inheritance tax should consider using up their other assets before withdrawing income from their pensions.

For example, after you have withdrawn your tax-free lump sum you could place the rest of your pension savings in a drawdown plan and leave most of it growing tax free for your family. You could then use your other assets to fund your retirement, e.g. rental properties and ISAs.

However, some financial advisors warn that if pension contributions are made with the primary intention of gaining an inheritance tax advantage, with no intention to save for retirement, the inheritance tax exemption is potentially open to challenge by HMRC.

It's impossible to say how big a risk this is and pension savers should continue to enjoy the succession planning possibilities associated with pensions. However, the primary purpose should be to save for retirement, not to save inheritance tax.

Of course, most retirees cannot afford to leave all their pension savings intact. But most will have at least some pension savings left to pass on to family members.

So for almost everyone it's good news that the 55% death tax has been abolished. It put some people off making significant pension contributions and put some retirees under pressure to withdraw income from their pensions as quickly as possible, with potentially adverse income tax consequences.

Minimising Tax on Withdrawals

Parents who wish to pass on their pension pots to their children may need to teach them how to withdraw money tax efficiently. For a pension to be an effective inter-generational tax shelter it's important your beneficiaries' withdrawals are taxed at 20% or less.

This isn't a problem if you die before age 75 because your beneficiaries (e.g. your children) will be able to withdraw the money tax free. However, there are still things they can do to produce a better financial outcome.

For example, if your children aren't worried about their own inheritance tax it may be more tax efficient for them to withdraw all the money tax free rather than pass on the pension pot to your grandchildren, who will have to pay income tax on their own withdrawals (if your children die after reaching age 75).

Your beneficiaries could also withdraw money from your pension pot to fund pension contributions of their own. With higher-rate tax relief this could leave them significantly better off overall.

If you die after reaching age 75 the withdrawals made by your beneficiaries will be taxed. However, tax-free withdrawals can be made if your beneficiaries have no other income and the withdrawals are covered by their income tax personal allowances (currently £11,500). This may be the case if they are at university, starting a business or taking time off work to raise children.

Withdrawals taxed at just 20% can be made while your beneficiaries are basic-rate taxpayers as long as their pension withdrawals do not take them over the higher-rate threshold – currently £45,000 (£43,000 in Scotland).

Example
Andrew, age 74, dies with £200,000 left in his pension plan. His wife Diane, age 70, is his beneficiary. She decides to keep the money in a drawdown plan so that it can continue to grow tax free and remains outside her estate for inheritance tax purposes. She withdraws a tax-free income of around £15,000 per year until she dies aged 80. At this point there is £150,000 left in the drawdown fund.

Until recently Diane's daughter Brenda was her nominated beneficiary. Brenda is a successful GP and a higher-rate taxpayer. If she inherits the pension pot she will pay 40% tax on any withdrawals.

So a few years ago Brenda encouraged Diane to nominate her two grandchildren as beneficiaries. They are currently aged 18 and 20 and at university. Thanks to Brenda's forward thinking, the grandchildren can withdraw tax-free income each year to use up their income tax personal allowances and help them through university. Then when they start working they can continue withdrawing money and may only pay tax at 20% if they are basic-rate taxpayers. Alternatively they can keep the remaining savings invested tax free until they need it, possibly when they themselves retire if they are extremely prudent!

Nominating Beneficiaries

It's important to make sure your pension provider has an up to date expression of wishes form which is simple to complete and is used to nominate who should get your pension savings when you die. They can be used to nominate more than one person.

If your beneficiaries aren't dependants and you have other dependants, your beneficiaries will only be able to use drawdown if you've nominated them. If there are no dependants and no nominees, the pension scheme can nominate anyone to receive drawdown.

Annuities

The rules are different if your pension savings have been used to buy an annuity – a secure income for life. See Chapter 12 for more details.

Chapter 10

How to Save Tax When You Tap Your Pension

When the pension rules were relaxed there were fears that retirees would blow their pension savings on expensive holidays and Lamborghinis. A few reckless individuals will no doubt squander their savings but the vast majority will probably withdraw the money gradually and spend it wisely.

Nevertheless, there is still a danger that even careful retirees will spend their savings a bit too quickly and end up depleting their pension pots.

Those who want a guaranteed income for life, with no danger of running out of money, can always hand over their retirement savings to an annuity provider. For example, a 65 year old with a £200,000 pension pot can currently buy a guaranteed income for life of around £5,000 per year. This income will increase in line with inflation and continue providing a pension for their widow.

It's not a lot but then again annuity rates are extremely low at present because interest rates are so low.

It may be possible to achieve a higher income by using a drawdown arrangement and investing in, for example, companies with a long track record of paying growing dividends, or other investments. However, your income will not be guaranteed and could fall, as could the value of your investments.

This is the dilemma retirees face in the wake of George Osborne's pension revolution. Freedom to spend your pension savings as you like does not necessarily buy you peace of mind.

You should probably only spend a tiny fraction of your pension savings each year if they are to last through your retirement. Some retirees may, however, wish to make bigger than normal withdrawals and this doesn't necessarily mean they're going to fritter the money away.

For example, you could use it to:

- Invest in tax-free ISAs
- Buy rental property
- Reduce your mortgage or other debts
- Start a business

However, one thing retirees no longer have to do is make bigger than normal pension withdrawals to avoid the 55% death tax (see Chapter 9). If anything, surplus money should remain invested in your pension pot for as long as possible so that it can be passed on to your family free from inheritance tax.

Tax will be an extremely important factor when it comes to deciding how much you withdraw from your pension and when. In this chapter we're going to take a closer look at some of the strategies pension savers may be able to follow to pay less income tax and capital gains tax.

For the first time, retirees have the freedom to control their tax bills to some extent, by making big pension withdrawals in some tax years and smaller withdrawals in others.

Saving Income Tax

Any money you withdraw from your pension, over and above your 25% tax-free lump sum, is subject to income tax. If you withdraw a lot in one go, you could end up paying tax at 40% or even 45%.

Most retirees should endeavour to pay no more than 20% tax on their pension withdrawals and one way to achieve this is by spreading withdrawals over many tax years.

During the current 2017/18 tax year, you pay no more than 20% tax if your taxable income from all sources is less than £45,000 (£43,000 in Scotland).

Most retirees do not, on average, earn more than £45,000 per year and should therefore refrain from making big pension withdrawals that push them into the 40% tax bracket.

Example

It's the start of the 2017/18 tax year. Andrew is 60 and earns a salary of £60,000. He has been saving into a personal pension and ISA. His pension pot is worth £200,000 and his ISA savings are worth £100,000. His wife Elizabeth is the same age and has similar income and savings.

If for whatever reason Andrew decided to withdraw all of his pension savings in one go, one quarter (£50,000) would be tax free. The remaining £150,000 would be fully taxed. His total taxable income would be £200,000 (£50,000 salary plus £150,000 pension).

With this much income, all of his pension withdrawal would be taxed at either 40% or 45%, plus he would lose his income tax personal allowance.

Andrew's total income tax bill would rise from £8,700 (salary only) to £75,800. He would up paying tax at an effective rate of 44.7% on his pension withdrawal.

Furthermore, the money he takes out would no longer grow tax free outside his pension plan.

Fortunately, Andrew has no need to tap his pension pot at this time and realizes he is better off leaving the money alone while he is working full time.

He doesn't even want to withdraw his tax-free lump sum because he has no use for it at present and wants it to continue growing tax free.

In fact, instead of taking money out, he intends to keep putting money into both his pension and ISA. He enjoys higher-rate tax relief on his pension contributions.

This is one of the reasons why pension savers need to be careful about tapping their savings too early. If you are using flexi-access drawdown and withdraw any income over and above your tax-free lump sum, your future pension contributions could be limited to just £4,000 per year (see Chapter 7).

A similar restriction applies if you withdraw any money as an uncrystallised funds pension lump sum (UFPLS).

Example continued

Three years later it's 2020/21 and Andrew is 63. He decides to resign from his job because he wants to work part time. His pension pot is now worth £270,000 and his ISA savings are worth £175,000. Before getting a part-time job he decides to take a year off to pursue various interests, including buying and renovating a rental property. Andrew and Elizabeth withdraw their 25% tax-free lump sums to purchase the property (£135,000 in total) and put the rest of their pension savings into drawdown plans.

Although the property will produce <u>taxable</u> income and capital gains (whereas the money was growing tax free inside their pensions), Andrew and Elizabeth believe they have found a genuine bargain which makes up for the loss of tax relief.

Because he has no other taxable income, Andrew decides to withdraw an additional amount of around £12,500 tax free from his pension to avoid wasting his personal allowance. He could also withdraw an extra £37,500 taxed at just 20% (the Government has promised to increase the personal allowance and basic-rate band to these levels by 2020/21).

Because he has withdrawn <u>income</u> from his pension, his future pension contributions will be limited to £4,000 per year. This does not cause Andrew any problems.

Example continued

A year later Andrew is 64 and gets a part-time job earning £15,000. He's also earning £5,000 rental income from his share of the property. If he doesn't need more income he can leave his pension pot to grow tax free. If he does want more income he can take at least another £30,000 taxed at just 20%.

Two years later Andrew is 66 and has reached state pension age and decides to stop working. His pension pot is now worth around £230,000 and his ISA savings have grown to over £200,000. Coupled with Elizabeth's savings and the income from the rental property, he feels financially secure enough to retire.

His state pension and rental income use up his income tax personal allowance so he will pay at least 20% tax on any income he withdraws from his pension in future. Keeping an eye on how his drawdown investments are performing, he varies the amount he withdraws each year but makes sure he never pays 40% income tax.

Reducing Capital Gains Tax

Because retirees can now choose how much money they withdraw from their pension pots each year, they can halt or reduce withdrawals in years they sell assets like rental property and reduce their capital gains tax bills.

This is because you only pay 18% capital gains tax (as opposed to 28%) to the extent your basic-rate band is not used up by your income*. For example, in 2017/18 if you don't have any taxable income you can have £33,500 of capital gains taxed at 18%.

The potential tax saving is £6,700 per couple:

$$£33,500 \times 2 \times 10\% = £6,700$$

* Note these are the capital gains tax rates for residential property. The rates for other assets are now 10% and 20% respectively.

Example continued

Several years later Andrew and Elizabeth decide to sell their rental property because it has increased in value significantly and they don't want the hassle of managing tenants etc. They intend to use the proceeds to buy a holiday cottage.

After deducting various buying and selling costs and their annual CGT exemptions they expect to be left with taxable capital gains of £30,000 each. These amounts will be taxed at just 18%, providing they haven't withdrawn too much income from their pension pots.

In the tax year before the sale takes place they therefore decide to make larger than normal pension withdrawals, making sure they stay below the higher-rate threshold to avoid paying 40% tax.

In the tax year in which the property is sold they reduce their pension withdrawals so that all of their capital gains are taxed at 18%. They live off the extra income they withdrew during the previous tax year.

Once the sale has taken place, and they know how much of their basic-rate bands are left, they can withdraw some additional money from their pension pots taxed at just 20%.

Leaving Pension Wealth to Your Family

When you die your remaining pension savings can be left to your family (e.g. your spouse or children) who can keep the money growing tax free and make withdrawals as and when they like. The withdrawals will be subject to income tax if you die after reaching age 75.

When it comes to leaving pension savings to adult children, it is no longer necessary to deplete your pension pot to avoid the 55% death tax.

ISA savings can also be left to family members but only your spouse can effectively keep them in the ISA tax wrapper. For spouses this is a new concession effective from 6 April 2015 (see Chapter 15).

Example continued

When Andrew dies at age 85 his remaining pension savings are left to Elizabeth. She also inherits his remaining ISA savings and is allowed to invest them in her own ISA.

Elizabeth now has two pension pots: her own and Andrew's. She wants to leave as much money as possible to her two children but she doesn't have to withdraw all her pension savings to avoid the 55% death tax.

Her remaining ISA savings can also be left to her children when she dies but the money will no longer be in a tax-free ISA and may be subject to inheritance tax.

One option would be to leave most of her pension savings intact and make tax-free withdrawals from her ISA to fund her living costs. This will reduce her estate for inheritance tax purposes.

If the children are likely to pay 40% income tax when they eventually inherit her pension savings, she could continue withdrawing income taxed at 20% in her hands and gift it to her children, although there may be inheritance tax consequences if she dies within seven years.

See the Taxcafe guide *How to Save Inheritance Tax* for more information about the various inheritance tax exemptions.

Withdrawing Lump Sums Gradually

Retirees who wish to make occasional large lump sum withdrawals should try to spread them over more than one tax year wherever possible.

Example
Barbara normally has taxable income of £30,000 made up of her state pension and withdrawals from her personal pension. In 2017/18 she wants to withdraw an additional £30,000 to pay for a new conservatory for her home in Bath. If she withdraws all the money in 2017/18, £15,000 will be taxed at 40%. If she withdraws the money over two tax years she will pay tax at just 20%. Her total tax saving will be £3,000.

Big Contributions Close to Retirement

Because retirees can now make unlimited pension withdrawals, it may be worth making bigger than normal pension contributions when you are close to retirement.

Example
Alan and Betty are both 60 and each earn £65,000 per year. At present, they make gross pension contributions of around £5,000 per year each.

Betty's mother recently passed away, leaving her £100,000. Betty decides to give half the money to Alan so they can both ramp up their pension contributions before they stop working in five years' time. The reason Betty gives half the money to Alan and the couple spread their increased contributions over five tax years is so that higher-rate tax relief can be enjoyed on all of the additional contributions (see Chapter 3).

They're happy to make these increased pension contributions in the knowledge that the money will not be locked up in any way – they will be able to withdraw as much as they like, whenever they like.

They personally invest an additional £50,000 each over a five year period, making sure they always invest just enough to maximise their higher-rate tax relief (see Chapter 3). For example, in 2017/18 they will make an additional gross pension contribution of £15,000 each:

£65,000 income - £45,000 higher-rate threshold - £5,000 existing contribution

This means a cash pension contribution of £12,000 (£15,000 x 0.8).

In total the taxman will add a total of £12,500 of basic-rate tax relief to each pension pot, so they end up with additional pension savings of £62,500 each. They also enjoy total tax refunds of £12,500 each when they submit their tax returns (their higher-rate tax relief).

Ignoring any tax-free investment growth they enjoy on these additional pension contributions, when they retire they'll each be able to withdraw an additional tax-free lump sum of £15,625 (£62,500 x 25%).

The remaining money (£46,875 each) will be fully taxed when withdrawn. If we assume the withdrawals are taxed at just 20%, Alan and Betty will each be left with £37,500. Depending on how much other income the couple have, these taxed withdrawals may have to be made over more than one tax year to avoid paying tax at 40%.

In total, Alan and Betty receive higher-rate tax relief of £25,000, tax-free lump sums totalling £31,250 and after-tax withdrawals totalling £75,000. So their £100,000 investment has grown to £131,250.

The reason Alan and Betty did so well is they spread their pension contributions over more than one tax year to maximize higher-rate tax relief and spread their withdrawals over more than one tax year to minimise their income tax bills.

It may also be worth making bigger pension contributions close to retirement even if you only enjoy basic-rate tax relief... but the benefits are far smaller.

Example

Emily is 60 and intends to retire next year. She earns a salary of £50,000 and in recent years has been investing just enough into her pension to maximise her higher-rate tax relief (see Chapter 3).

She has £24,000 sitting in a savings account and decides to invest all of it in her pension. The taxman adds £6,000 of basic-rate tax relief so she ends up with additional pension savings of £30,000. There is no higher-rate tax relief on this additional contribution.

Soon after retiring she decides to withdraw the whole £30,000. One quarter (£7,500) will be tax free. Emily pays 20% tax on the remaining £22,500, leaving her with £18,000. In total, Emily is left with £25,500, compared with her original investment of £24,000. So she enjoys a £1,500 windfall from this simple piece of tax planning.

What the above examples reveal is that, where possible, pension contributions should always be spread over several tax years if this means more higher-rate tax relief can be enjoyed.

Big pension contributions that only result in basic-rate tax relief may still be worthwhile in some cases but the benefits are modest.

You also have to watch out for HMRC's recycling rules. These are designed to stop you taking a tax-free lump sum and reinvesting it in your pension with a second round of tax relief (see Chapter 8).

The recycling rules can also be triggered if you make big pension contributions in the two tax years *before* you start withdrawing money.

HMRC says that very few lump sums will be affected and the recycling rules are only triggered if you always intended your tax-free lump sum to be an integral part of paying for your increased contributions (either directly or indirectly).

Retirees with Other Income

Retirees who are currently basic-rate taxpayers but expect to become higher-rate taxpayers in the near future, may consider making bigger pension withdrawals now to avoid paying tax at 40% in future.

Why would you expect to become a higher-rate taxpayer? Perhaps if you expect to receive a windfall (e.g. an inheritance) or expect your income to grow faster than inflation.

Example
Ann is 75 and widowed and has income of £20,000 from her state pension and some rental properties. She also has a personal pension pot worth £200,000 from which she withdraws roughly £10,000 per year. Her total income is £30,000 so she only pays 20% tax.

Her mother Betty is 95 and lives in a nursing home. Ann expects to inherit all of Betty's assets when she dies, giving her additional taxable income of roughly £30,000 per year. With this extra income Ann will become a higher-rate taxpayer and will effectively pay 40% tax on the income she withdraws from her pension.

Before Betty dies Ann decides to withdraw an additional £10,000 per year from her pension and invest the money in an ISA where it will continue to grow tax free. She reasons that it is better to pay an additional £2,000 per year income tax now rather than £4,000 per year at some point in the future as a higher-rate taxpayer.

Although Ann may save income tax by making bigger pension withdrawals before becoming a higher-rate taxpayer, she may end up aggravating a more significant long-term tax problem she faces – inheritance tax.

When Ann eventually dies, 40% inheritance tax could be payable on a significant chunk of her assets: her rental properties, the money she inherited from her mother and the additional money she withdrew from her pension and invested in an ISA.

She'll be able to leave her remaining pension savings to her children or grandchildren free from inheritance tax, although they will pay income tax on any money they withdraw, possibly at 40% or more.

Ann could therefore consider gifting the additional money she withdraws from her pension to her children or grandchildren rather than invest it in an ISA.

Alternatively, she could consider halting all withdrawals from her pension after she inherits her mother's assets. This will allow her to avoid paying income tax at 40% and leave a bigger pension pot for her family to inherit.

Retirees with significant assets face a difficult juggling act deciding how much income to withdraw from their pensions to save both income tax and inheritance tax.

However, now that the 55% pension death tax has been scrapped they have considerably more flexibility and don't need to deplete their pension savings quickly.

Summary

- It is now possible to make unlimited pension withdrawals when you reach pension age (55 or 57 but possibly older).

- Any money you withdraw, over and above your tax-free lump sum, will be subject to income tax.

- Most retirees pay no more than 20% tax and should avoid making withdrawals taxed at 40% or even 45%.

- This can be achieved by spreading withdrawals over many tax years, while keeping an eye on the higher-rate threshold (£45,000 in 2017/18, £43,000 in Scotland).

- Taxable lump sum withdrawals should be spread over more than one tax year where practical.

- In most cases it will not be tax efficient to withdraw income if you are still working and a higher-rate taxpayer.

- In some cases it may be worth postponing withdrawals so that capital gains are taxed at 18% instead of 28%.

- Money left inside your pension pot when you die is generally not subject to inheritance tax and is no longer subject to the 55% death tax.

- Your remaining pension savings can be left to anyone, e.g. your children or grandchildren. The money will continue to grow tax free but income tax will be paid on any withdrawals they make (unless you die before age 75).

Chapter 11

Pensions versus Buy-to-Let

Should you withdraw money from your pension to buy property?

This may be a good idea if you can earn a better *after-tax* return from property than from your *tax-free* pension investments (typically shares and bonds).

Investing in property has, however, become less attractive following two recent tax announcements:

- A 3% increase in stamp duty land tax
- A restriction to mortgage interest tax relief

Prior to April 2016 you wouldn't have paid any stamp duty land tax if you bought a rental property for £100,000... now you'll pay £3,000. You would have paid just £2,500 stamp duty if you bought a property for £250,000... now you'll pay £10,000!

When you add legal fees and mortgage arrangement fees, buying investment property is much more expensive than buying shares. With shares the stamp duty is just 0.5% and brokers' commission is often no more than a few pounds.

Thanks to the second tax change borrowing to invest in property is becoming much more expensive for many landlords. The restriction to interest tax relief will prove even more painful than the stamp duty increase because those affected will feel its impact every year, not just when a new rental property is purchased.

Higher-rate tax relief for interest and other finance is being phased out over a four year period commencing with the current 2017/18 tax year. Instead landlords will be allowed a "tax reduction" equivalent to just 20% of their finance costs.

The tax relief restriction will only affect *residential* property businesses and the new rules will not apply to properties held inside companies.

See the Taxcafe guide *Landlord Interest* for more information.

Example

Hannah is 55, a higher-rate taxpayer and has a pension pot worth £85,000. She decides to withdraw all the money to pay the deposits on two buy-to-let properties which she thinks will perform better than her pension investments over the next 10 years.

The first 25% she withdraws is tax free and the rest is taxed at 40%, leaving her with a grand total of £59,500. Using buy-to-let mortgages she acquires two properties for £100,000 each, with a £25,000 deposit and £75,000 mortgage on each property. The final £9,500 of her pension savings is used to cover her purchase costs (including stamp duty land tax of £6,000 and legal fees).

To be conservative we'll assume that, on average over the period, she doesn't make any rental profits – all her rental income goes towards paying mortgage interest, income tax and other expenses. This assumption builds in a possible increase in interest rates and takes account of the restriction to mortgage interest tax relief.

We'll also assume Hannah's properties grow by roughly 7% per year. 10 years' later, when she's 65, they're worth £400,000 in total. She decides to sell one property to pay off both mortgages and use the second property for retirement income. On the £200,000 property she sells she faces a capital gains tax bill of roughly £20,000. After paying off both mortgages (£150,000 in total) she's left with £30,000 in the bank and a fully paid up property worth £200,000.

How would she have fared by keeping her pension investments instead? If we assume they also would have grown by roughly 7% per year, after 10 years she'd end up with around £170,000. She could withdraw 25% tax free and, assuming the rest was withdrawn gradually and taxed at just 20%, she would end up with £144,500 in total.

In summary, with property she ends up with £230,000, with a pension she ends up with £144,500.

Hannah does much better with property despite paying 40% tax on all the money she takes out of her pension to fund the purchases and despite the fact that she does not enjoy any rental profit and pays capital gains tax when she sells one of the properties.

Of course, the only reason the properties did better is because they were heavily geared up with borrowed money and grew handsomely in value. This is a very high-risk strategy and probably only suitable for experienced property investors who are many years away from retirement (i.e. closer to 55 than 65).

If the properties had fallen in value, Hannah could have lost all of her capital.

What about using your pension savings to invest in property without buy-to-let mortgages? Let's take a look at a simple example:

Example
Bill is 65 and retired and has a pension pot worth £150,000 (he has already taken his tax-free lump sum), as well as other taxable income of roughly £20,000 per year.

He currently withdraws the income generated by his pension investments but wants to keep the capital intact for his children. His pension savings are invested in an equity income fund earning income of £5,250 per year (£4,200 after paying 20% income tax). He wants to know if he could get more income by withdrawing all the money from his pension and buying a rental property outright without a mortgage.

If he withdraws all his pension pot in one go he'll pay 40% income tax on most of the money. He will also lose his personal allowance and some of the money will be taxed at 45%. So we'll assume he withdraws £50,000 per year over three tax years, paying 20% tax on around half his withdrawals and 40% tax on the rest, leaving him with £105,000.

He then buys a rental property for £100,000, using the final £5,000 to cover his stamp duty and legal fees. If the property is to earn more income than his pension investments (£5,250) it will need a rental yield of more than 5.25%. That's ignoring empty periods and the additional costs he will incur including repairs, insurance, letting agent fees etc.

It is possible to find properties with higher rental yields (in some parts of the country they are higher, in others parts they are lower) but it's probably unlikely Bill will end up with *significantly* more income after deducting the various expenses he will incur.

The problem with using pension savings to buy an expensive asset like property outright is that it may be necessary to spread the withdrawals over many tax years to avoid paying income tax at 40% or more.

And what about Bill's children? When he dies they'll either inherit a pension pot worth £150,000 or a property worth £100,000, plus any capital growth on the investments. Whether they're better off with a pension pot or property will depend on Bill's inheritance tax status and the amount of income tax the children pay.

Let's say Bill's pension pot would be worth £225,000 when he dies after reaching age 75 and his property would be worth £150,000 (i.e. they would both grow by 50%).

If Bill's property is not subject to inheritance tax, his children will inherit the £150,000 asset outright, with no capital gains tax payable if they sell it immediately. Alternatively they will inherit his £225,000 pension pot with income tax payable on any withdrawals, leaving them with either £180,000 (if they pay 20% income tax) or £135,000 (if they pay 40% income tax).

If Bill's property is subject to 40% inheritance tax, his children will inherit £90,000. No inheritance tax would be payable on his pension savings, which means the children will, as before, be left with either £180,000 (after paying 20% income tax) or £135,000 (after paying 40% income tax).

In this example the children are only better off with the property if there is no inheritance tax payable and they pay income tax at 40%. Of course, they wouldn't have to withdraw the pension savings immediately. The money could be left to grow tax free for as long as they like, perhaps until they themselves retire.

In summary, it is now possible to deplete your pension savings to invest in property. However, this strategy is only likely to leave you better off if you're prepared to accept more risk (i.e. borrow money) or you expect property to deliver significantly higher returns than pension investments (typically shares and bonds).

Chapter 12

Drawdown versus Annuities

When you retire you may prefer to use your retirement savings to buy an annuity, rather than use flexi-access drawdown (see Chapter 7).

Annuities get a bad rap in the press but offer one important benefit: a guaranteed income for life. This may appeal to older retirees who don't want the hassle of managing investments and desire what is as close as it gets to a risk-free income.

Annuity rates are very low at present but may improve if interest rates increase from their current historic lows. Having said this, they may become even less attractive in future if only a small minority of retirees buy them (those who expect to live a long time).

Annuities are seen by many as a con. The idea is lots of retirees pool their money together and those that live longer than average are subsidized by those who live shorter than average. That's fair enough but what many people suspect is that annuity providers (typically insurance companies) skim off a big chunk of the money for themselves.

There are several other reasons why flexi-access drawdown may be more attractive than buying an annuity immediately:

Benefit #1 – Take the Tax-free Cash and Keep Working

When you reach age 55 you may want to get your hands on your 25% tax-free lump sum but keep working for another 10 years or even longer.

Any additional income you take from your pension pot while you are still working (e.g. annuity income) could be taxed at 40% or more if you also have income from a job or business.

Because there is no requirement to withdraw income from a flexi-access drawdown arrangement, you can postpone withdrawing income until you actually retire and your income tax rate falls.

While you are working your pension savings will continue to grow tax free.

Benefit #2 – Keep Your Favourite Investments

If you opt for an annuity you generally have to sell your pension investments and hand over your savings to an insurance company.

This is not an attractive proposition if you are confident your pension investments will perform well.

With a drawdown pension you can enjoy the best of both worlds: an income and tax-free investment growth on the money left inside your pension.

Benefit #3 – Wait for Better Annuity Rates

Many pension experts argue that you should ultimately use your pension savings to buy an annuity because the income is more secure than drawdown income (the income never falls no matter how long you live and no matter what happens to interest rates and the value of investments).

The problem is that annuity rates may be very low when you retire if interest rates are very low, as they are now. One solution is to start your retirement with a drawdown pension and make a phased exit by using part of your drawdown money to buy an annuity at regular intervals if interest rates rise and annuities become more attractive.

Benefit #4 – Reduce Your Income and Save Tax

If you can vary your income from year to year, as you can with drawdown, you can do a lot of constructive tax planning. This is very useful in years when your tax bill may spike because you receive big one-off receipts such as capital gains.

Let's say you sell a buy-to-let property and the capital gain is £50,000. If you reduce your drawdown income in the same tax year, so that your basic-rate band is not fully utilised, you will pay 18% tax instead of 28% tax on a big chunk of your capital gain.

The basic-rate band for 2017/18 is £33,500 so the maximum potential tax saving from paying 18% capital gains tax instead of 28% tax is currently:

$$£33,500 \times 10\% = £3,350$$

This tax saving could be enjoyed every time you sell a rental property and allows individuals with many properties to wind down their portfolios slowly when they retire.

Further capital gains tax savings can be achieved by spreading property sales across several tax years because this lets you make use of more than one annual CGT exemption. The potential additional tax saving in 2017/18 is £3,164 (£11,300 x 28%).

Annuities after Death

If you are receiving income from a bog-standard annuity, no money will be payable to your family (e.g. your children) after you die.

The income payments will continue if you have purchased a joint-life annuity (typically for your spouse) or an annuity which pays out for a guaranteed period.

The tax treatment has become more generous since 6 April 2015. If you die before age 75, payments made to your beneficiary will be tax free.

If you die when you are 75 or older, income paid to your beneficiary will be taxed at their marginal rate.

Part 3
Pensions vs ISAs

Chapter 13

Introduction

Which is better: an ISA or a pension?

This is an important question. ISAs and pensions are the two most popular savings vehicles for individuals.

When it comes to saving tax there are no ifs, buts or maybes: pensions are a **<u>much</u>** more powerful tax shelter.

With ISAs there is no up-front tax relief on the money you put in but withdrawals are tax free. With pensions there is up-front tax relief but most withdrawals are taxed.

At first glance the two tax reliefs appear quite different but, as it happens, tax-free withdrawals (ISAs) and up-front tax relief (pensions), produce exactly the same result, even though the tax savings are enjoyed at different points in time.

However, there are two reasons why pensions are a much better tax shelter:

- **The tax-free lump sum**. Not all of your pension withdrawals are taxed. You can take one quarter as a tax-free lump sum.

- **Retirees pay less tax**. If your tax rate falls from 40% to 20% when you retire – as with most higher-rate taxpayers – a pension will save you more tax than an ISA. Tax-free ISA withdrawals are only as good as tax-relief on pension contributions IF your income tax rate does not fall when you retire.

Thanks to these two factors, it is quite possible that a pension will generate 42% more after-tax income than an ISA, as we shall see in the next chapter.

Other Tax Differences

Apart from these major tax differences, pensions and ISAs are treated differently in other respects which may be important in some circumstances.

Interest on Cash Balances

While it has always been possible to hold cash in a stocks and shares ISA, any interest was in effect paid net of basic-rate tax. Interest earned in a pension has always been tax free.

Since July 2014 this has changed. Interest on cash held in a stocks and shares ISA is now completely tax-free.

Tax When You Emigrate

If you become non-UK resident your income and capital gains sheltered inside an ISA will continue to be tax free. Tax free in the UK, that is. The amounts may be taxed in your new country of residence. For example, the Isle of Man Government specifically states in its tax return booklet that an ISA's tax-free status "does not apply in the Isle of Man and you should declare any income from these products".

The tax-exempt status of pensions, on the other hand, is recognized in most countries, although they are arguably less portable assets (you can withdraw all your ISA savings easily if you emigrate).

Withholding Taxes on Dividends

These days it is easy for stock market investors to buy shares in overseas companies, the most popular being US companies. You have to be careful about doing this because the dividends are often subject to a withholding tax.

In the US, the dividend withholding tax rate is 30%. However, in terms of the double tax agreement between the US and UK, the amount of withholding tax can be reduced by completing an IRS form W-8BEN. Most online stockbrokers will handle these forms on your behalf so the process is relatively simple.

However, there is an important difference between US shares held inside a pension and an ISA. The double tax agreement provides a specific exemption for pension schemes, which means US dividends can be received tax free by UK pension savers.

The double tax agreement does not, however, recognize ISAs. ISA investors are subject to the same reduced withholding tax rate as everyone else: 15%.

ISAs – Protection from Greedy Politicians

Although pensions are a better tax shelter, one tax benefit unique to ISAs is protection from future increases in income tax rates.

Money withdrawn from ISAs is tax free, whether those withdrawals take place next year or in 30 years' time. In contrast, if a future UK Government (or Scottish Government if you live north of the border) decides to increase income tax rates or reduce the threshold where 40% tax kicks in, it is quite possible that you will pay more than 20% tax on the money you withdraw from a pension.

It is impossible to predict what will happen to income tax rates in the years ahead. However, there's no denying that Britain has had its fair share of barmy taxes. In 1974, the top income tax rate on earnings was increased to 83% and the top rate on investment income was 98%.

Do you trust politicians to not increase your income tax at any time between now and the date you die? If not, then it may be a good idea to put some of your retirement savings into ISAs.

ISAs are not, however, completely immune from politicians. There have been rumours in the press in recent times about a lifetime cap being placed on ISA savings to limit the number of 'ISA millionaires.' Nothing has been announced to date.

Help-to-Buy ISA

In the 2015 Budget George Osborne introduced the Help to Buy ISA – a form of cash ISA where the Government adds £50 for every £200 you save towards a deposit for a first property. The maximum Government bonus is £3,000 for those who save £12,000.

Each person can have a Help to Buy ISA, so those buying together can each have a separate Help to Buy ISA, with a total of £6,000 of free cash from the Government.

Essentially the Government bonus is equivalent to the 20% tax relief basic-rate taxpayers enjoy on their pension contributions.

You can open an account up until 30 November 2019 and keep contributing until 30 November 2029.

An initial deposit of £1,200 can be made when the Help to Buy ISA is first opened. Thereafter the maximum monthly saving permitted is £200.

Savers can withdraw funds from their account if they need them for another purpose but the bonus will only be made available to buy a home.

Help to Buy ISAs are available through banks and building societies to individuals (minimum age 16) who are first-time home buyers. They can be used to purchase, as a personal residence, a first home worth up to £450,000 in London or £250,000 elsewhere in the UK.

Each ISA provider can apply their own withdrawal rules and set their own interest rates.

As is currently the case, it will only be possible to subscribe to one cash ISA per year. It will therefore not be possible to subscribe to a Help to Buy ISA with one provider and another cash ISA with a different provider.

The one potential downside is investment choice. The Help to Buy ISA is a cash ISA and the stocks and shares option has been omitted which may put off some long-term savers who want to take more risk to achieve better returns.

Lifetime ISA

Those aged 18 to 39 can open a Lifetime ISA which can be used to save for a first home or for retirement.

Any money you put in (up to £4,000 per year) receives a 25% Government bonus. So if you put in £4,000, the Government will add £1,000.

It's possible to continue making contributions up to age 50. This means you will be able to invest up to £128,000 between age 18 and 50 with a Government bonus of up to £32,000.

During the 2017/18 tax year the bonus will be added at the end of the tax year. From 2018/19 onwards the bonus will be paid monthly.

Contributions to a Lifetime ISA fall within the overall £20,000 ISA subscription limit. In other words, if you invest £4,000 in your Lifetime ISA you will be able to invest another £16,000 in a cash ISA or a stocks and shares ISA.

Lifetime ISAs are available from banks, building societies and investment managers and qualifying investments are the same as for cash ISAs and stocks and shares ISAs.

You can open more than one Lifetime ISA during your lifetime (as long you're under 40) but can only pay into one during each tax year.

Lifetime ISAs – Early Withdrawals

Unlike a pension, your savings are not locked up inside a Lifetime ISA.

However, if you withdraw money before reaching age 60, for any reason other than to buy your first home, there will be a 25% early withdrawal charge.

This will claw back all of the Government bonus, plus an additional 6.25% of the amount you invested.

For example, if you invest £1,000, the Government will add £250, giving you total savings of £1,250. If you then decide to withdraw the money, the 25% penalty will be £312.50, leaving you with £937.50.

Thus you will lose the Government bonus plus an extra £62.50 (6.25%) out of the amount you originally invested.

This charge will also effectively apply to any growth in the value of your savings.

For the 2017/18 tax year only, where any withdrawal is made the Lifetime ISA will be closed and there will be no early withdrawal charge. It will still be possible to open a new Lifetime ISA during 2017/18 and contribute a further £4,000.

Where an individual is diagnosed with terminal ill health, they will be able to withdraw all their Lifetime ISA savings tax free (including the bonus), regardless of age.

Lifetime ISAs – Buying Your First Home

If you use your Lifetime ISA to buy your first home, funds can be withdrawn 12 months after opening the account. The property must cost no more than £450,000, be located in the UK and your only residence.

You will not be able to use the money to invest in buy-to-let property.

The account holder will inform their ISA manager that a property is to be purchased and the funds will be paid direct to the solicitor.

As well as saving in a Lifetime ISA, it will be possible to open a Help to Buy ISA until 30 November 2019 and keep contributing until 30 November 2029.

However, you will only be able to use the Government bonus from one of the accounts to buy your first home.

If you have a Help to Buy ISA and a Lifetime ISA you could, for example:

- Use the Help to Buy ISA with the Government bonus to buy your first home and keep your Lifetime ISA to save for retirement

- Use the Lifetime ISA with the Government bonus to buy your first home and withdraw the money in your Help to Buy ISA (without the government bonus) to also fund the purchase

During the 2017/18 tax year only, those who already have a Help to Buy ISA will be able to transfer their savings into a Lifetime ISA and receive the Government bonus on those savings at the end of the tax year.

Transfers of money saved prior to the introduction of the Lifetime ISA on 6 April 2017 will not count towards the £4,000 Lifetime ISA contribution limit.

Lifetime ISAs – Saving for Retirement

If you use your Lifetime ISA to save for retirement, funds can be withdrawn from age 60.

As we shall see in the next chapter, a Lifetime ISA could be an attractive alternative to saving in a pension if you are a basic-rate taxpayer. Like pensions they will attract a top up from the Government but, unlike pensions, ALL the money you take out will be tax free.

However, in most cases it would probably be unwise to stop making contributions to a workplace pension scheme because that would also mean giving up your employer's contribution (which is effectively 'free' money).

The Lifetime ISA will have the same inheritance tax treatment as other ISAs: when you die the funds will form part of your estate for inheritance tax purposes.

However, your spouse will be able to transfer all your ISA savings into their own ISA so that the money continues to grow tax free.

ISAs – Non-tax Benefits

- **Flexibility**. ISAs are extremely flexible investments that allow you to access your savings *at any time*. From 6 April 2016 you can withdraw and replace cash from your ISA without it counting towards your annual ISA subscription limit, as long as the repayment is made in the same tax year as the withdrawal. Pension savers can only access their money when they reach age 55 or 57 (potentially later in future). It's a fat lot of good having £100,000 sitting in your pension pot if you desperately need emergency cash.

- **No age limit**. You cannot keep contributing to a pension indefinitely. Once you reach age 75 you have to stop. There is no upper age limit for ISA investments and you can withdraw money and make new contributions continually.

- **No earnings required**. If you want to contribute more than £3,600 per year to a pension you need 'earnings'. There is no such restriction on ISA investments, although the maximum annual investment is currently capped at £20,000.

Pensions – Non-tax Benefits

- **Investment limits**. The maximum annual pension investment is currently £40,000 and the carry-forward rules allow a contribution of up to £160,000. However, as we saw in Chapter 3, the maximum contribution that you can make with full higher-rate tax relief is probably a lot lower than these limits.

- **Investment choice**. Pensions offer a wider choice of investments than ISAs. For example, ISAs cannot be used to invest directly in commercial property whereas pensions can.

- **Protection from creditors**. In the event of bankruptcy, your savings in an HMRC approved pension cannot be claimed by your creditors. (Most occupational and personal pensions are HMRC approved.) Pension withdrawals can, however, be grabbed if they take place before you are discharged from bankruptcy.

Chapter 14

Case Study: ISA vs Pension

In this chapter we'll follow two investors building up a retirement nest egg over 10 years and see who ends up better off:

- Peter – Pension investor
- Ian – ISA investor

Both are higher-rate taxpayers and invest £6,000 per year. Peter makes an initial contribution of £8,000 to which the taxman adds a further £2,000 in basic-rate tax relief.

He then claims back £2,000 when completing his tax return. All in all Peter has £10,000 of pension savings that have only cost him £6,000.

Ian also invests £6,000 per year out of his own pocket in an ISA. He doesn't get any tax relief on his contributions so his total investment is just £6,000. Note Ian invests in a traditional ISA. We'll compare pensions and Lifetime ISAs shortly.

Both Peter and Ian enjoy investment returns of 7% per year. These returns are completely tax free for both the ISA investor and the pension investor.

We track how both investors perform from year to year in Table 2. At the end of year 1 they have £10,700 and £6,420 respectively, which is simply their initial investments of £10,000 and £6,000 plus 7% tax-free investment growth.

After five years, Peter has £24,613 more than Ian and after 10 years he has £59,134 more than Ian. Even though they're both earning an identical tax-free return of 7% and investing the same amount of money out of their own pockets, Peter is much better off because his annual investment is boosted by income tax relief on his contributions.

In fact, Ian always has just 60% as much money as Peter. Peter's extra 40% is thanks to the income tax relief he receives on his pension contributions.

Table 2
Pension Savings vs ISA Savings

End Year	Pension £	ISA £
1	10,700	6,420
2	22,149	13,289
3	34,399	20,640
4	47,507	28,504
5	61,533	36,920
6	76,540	45,924
7	92,598	55,559
8	109,780	65,868
9	128,164	76,899
10	147,836	88,702

After-tax Comparison

Although Ian's retirement savings are much smaller than Peter's, that's not the whole story. Firstly, Ian enjoyed much more flexibility along the way and could have taken money out of his ISA at any time. Peter can only withdraw money from his pension when he's 55 or older.

Secondly, Ian can withdraw all his ISA savings *tax-free*. Peter will have to pay income tax on any money he withdraws over and above his 25% tax-free lump sum.

If he withdraws all his pension savings in one go, he'll end up paying tax at 40% on most of the money. However, because these are *retirement savings*, we will assume that Peter only withdraws a little bit of money each year to avoid depleting his capital too quickly and therefore pays income tax at 20%.

But before we do this let's pretend Peter has to pay 40% tax on all his pension withdrawals and the pension rules do not allow for tax-free lump sums. How do ISAs and pensions compare then?

40% Tax, No Tax-Free Lump Sum

After paying 40% tax on all of his withdrawals Peter the pension saver will be left with £88,702:

$$£147,836 \text{ less } 40\% \text{ tax} = £88,702$$

Ian the ISA investor will also be left with £88,702:

$$£88,702 \text{ less } 0\% \text{ tax} = £88,702$$

As you can see, their after-tax positions are *identical*. As I pointed out in the previous chapter, if you are a higher-rate taxpayer both before and after you retire, and ignoring the tax-free lump sum, ISAs and pensions offer identical tax savings.

Peter may have received 40% income tax relief on the money he put in but he also has to pay 40% tax on the money he takes out. This puts him back in the same position as Ian the ISA investor.

40% Tax, Tax-Free Lump Sum

Of course, in practice Peter can take a 25% tax-free lump sum of £36,959 (£147,836 x 25%). He'll only pay tax on the remaining £110,877.

If we assume he still pays 40% tax on the rest of his pension withdrawals his position after tax is as follows:

Tax-free lump sum: £36,959
After-tax income (£110,877 less 40% tax):   £66,526

Peter is left with a total of £103,485 compared with Ian the ISA investor's £88,702.

This means Peter has approximately 17% more money.

So even if you're a higher-rate taxpayer when you retire you will still receive more after-tax income from a pension than an ISA, thanks to the tax-free lump sum. Although most retirees are basic-rate taxpayers, you could end up paying tax at 40% on some or all of your pension withdrawals if you have a significant amount of income from other sources, e.g. rental property.

20% Tax, Tax-Free Lump Sum

Finally, we'll assume that Peter, like most other retirees, is a basic-rate taxpayer when he retires. Peter's after-tax position is now as follows:

Tax-free lump sum: £36,959
After-tax income (£110,877 less 20% tax):   £88,702

Peter is left with a total of £125,661 compared with Ian the ISA investor's £88,702.

Peter the pension saver ends up with 42% more money than Ian the ISA investor.

This example shows that, if you are a higher-rate taxpayer while you are saving for retirement and a basic-rate taxpayer when you retire, you will end up significantly better off using a pension rather than an ISA to save for retirement.

Tax-Free Pension Withdrawals

In the above example Peter pays 20% income tax on all of his pension income. The implicit assumption is that his income tax personal allowance is used up by other taxable income, perhaps his state pension and income from rental properties or a part-time job or part-time business.

I taxed all of his private pension income because I did not want to overstate the benefits of pension saving. In reality, some of the income you receive from a private pension plan may be tax free thanks to your income tax personal allowance.

The income tax personal allowance for the current 2017/18 tax year is £11,500 and will increase to £12,500 by 2020/21.

There used to be additional age-related personal allowances for older taxpayers but these have now been almost completely phased out.

Nevertheless, the sharp increase in the standard income tax personal allowance in recent years means that most retirees will continue to receive a significant proportion of their income tax free.

Once you reach state pension age your state pension will use up a big chunk of your personal allowance. However, you can start receiving income from your other pensions up to 10 years earlier. If during this period your taxable income from other sources (e.g. rental property) does not use up all of your personal allowance, some of your pension income will be tax free.

If some of your pension income will be tax-free, this makes pensions even more attractive than ISAs for retirement saving.

Lifetime ISA vs Pension

Those aged 18 to 39 can now open a Lifetime ISA which can be used to save for a first home or for retirement.

It's possible to invest up to £4,000 per year with a 25% Government bonus and continue contributing up to age 50.

The Lifetime ISA is an attractive alternative to saving in a pension if you are a basic-rate taxpayer. Like pensions they attract a top up from the Government but, unlike pensions, ALL the money you take out will be tax free.

For example, if you are a basic-rate taxpayer and invest £1,000 in either a pension or a Lifetime ISA you will receive a £250 top up from the taxman, leaving you with £1,250 in either account.

When you retire, however, withdrawals from the Lifetime ISA will be tax free, whereas only 25% of the money withdrawn from the pension will be tax free. The rest will typically be taxed at 20% (if you are a basic-rate taxpayer when you retire).

If we ignore investment growth to keep the example simple (it doesn't affect the outcome), with a Lifetime ISA you will end up with £1,250, with a pension you will end up with just £1,063 after tax.

Thus, if you're a basic-rate taxpayer, your retirement income will be 17.6% higher with a Lifetime ISA!

Lifetime ISA vs Pension – Higher-rate Taxpayers

Higher-rate taxpayers will generally get more bang for their buck with a pension.

For example, if you invest £1,000 in a Lifetime ISA you will receive a £250 top up from the Government leaving you with £1,250.

However, because higher-rate taxpayers also receive a tax refund when they contribute to a pension (higher-rate tax relief) they can make bigger initial contributions. For example, if you invest £1,333 in a pension (£1,000/0.75) you'll receive a £333 top up from the Government, leaving you with £1,666 in your pension.

You will also receive higher-rate relief of £333 (£1,666 x 20%) so, as with a Lifetime ISA, the investment will only cost you £1,000 personally (£1,333 personal investment - £333 higher-rate relief).

Ignoring investment growth, when you retire your £1,666 pension pot will become £1,416 (after taking 25% tax free and the rest taxed at 20%), compared with the £1,250 you would receive from a Lifetime ISA.

Thus, your retirement income could be 13% higher with a pension.

But if you are still a higher-rate taxpayer when you retire (for example if you have a lot of income from other sources, e.g. rental property) you will end up with only £1,166 from a pension, compared with £1,250 from a Lifetime ISA. Thus your retirement income could be 7% higher with a Lifetime ISA.

There are other important differences between Lifetime ISAs and pensions. With a pension your money is completely locked up until you are 55 (rising to 57 in 2028). With a Lifetime ISA you will lose the Government top up and pay a penalty if you withdraw anything before age 60, unless the money is used to buy your first home. The rest of your savings can be withdrawn at any time.

If the pension is a company scheme, the additional contribution from your employer will make investing in such a scheme more attractive than a Lifetime ISA in most circumstances. In other words, you should probably not opt out of your employer's pension scheme to invest in a Lifetime ISA.

Make Mine a Double!

It *may* be possible to invest in a Lifetime ISA and then, when you're 60, take the money out and stick it into a pension, thereby enjoying two rounds of tax relief.

For example, if you invest £1,000 in a Lifetime ISA you will receive a 25% Government bonus, leaving you with £1,250. Ignoring investment growth, when you're 60 you will be able to withdraw the £1,250 tax free and may be able to invest it in a pension.

Because higher-rate taxpayers also receive a tax refund when they contribute to a pension (higher-rate tax relief), they can make bigger initial contributions. So instead of investing just your Lifetime ISA savings of £1,250 in your pension, you may be able to invest £1,667 (£1,250/0.75).

You'll receive £417 of basic-rate tax relief from the taxman, leaving you with £2,084 in your pension. You will also receive higher-rate relief of £417 (£2,084 x 20%), so the investment will only cost you £1,250 personally (the amount withdrawn from the Lifetime ISA).

Ignoring investment growth, when you eventually retire your £2,084 pension pot will become £1,771 (after taking 25% tax free and the rest taxed at 20%), compared with the £1,250 you would receive from your Lifetime ISA alone.

Thus, your retirement income could be 42% higher than someone who invests in a Lifetime ISA only.

And your retirement income will be 77% higher than someone who invests in a traditional ISA only (ignoring investment growth they would end up with just £1,000).

It's impossible to say whether anyone will be able to benefit from this potential "tax loophole".

Because only those who are under 40 can open a Lifetime ISA and because withdrawals will only be possible from age 60, it will be over 20 years before anyone can perform this tax relief double! Tax and pension rules will no doubt change a lot between now and then.

Chapter 15

ISAs vs Pensions: Death Tax Planning

Your Spouse

There is no inheritance tax on assets, including ISAs, left to your spouse.

Thanks to a recent change that applies from 6 April 2015, your spouse can now inherit your ISA savings and invest them in their own ISA, so any future income and capital gains will continue to be tax free.

This was not possible before – your spouse could inherit your ISA savings but they were taken out of the ISA wrapper.

What happens now is your spouse will receive a special expanded ISA allowance when you die which will allow them to put all your ISA savings into their own ISA.

This tax concession is available to married couples and civil partners but not common-law spouses (i.e. unmarried couples).

How do ISAs compare with pensions?

Your spouse or common-law spouse can inherit your pension pot and withdraw money from it as and when they like. The investments inside the pension will continue to grow tax free.

If you die before age 75 your spouse or common-law spouse can withdraw all the money tax free. If you die after reaching age 75 they will pay income tax on any money they take out.

If your spouse or common-law spouse already has significant pension savings or other taxable income of their own and inherits a second pension pot from you, it is possible that any additional withdrawals they make from the second pension pot will take them over the higher-rate threshold and be taxed at 40%.

For this reason it may be preferable, in some cases, for married couples to run down their pension savings rather than their ISA savings, as long as no more than 20% tax is paid on the pension withdrawals.

The surviving spouse can then inherit a larger quantity of ISA savings and make tax-free withdrawals from them.

Unmarried couples who inherit ISA savings cannot keep them inside the tax wrapper. This means they may pay tax on any *future* income and capital gains. However, the original capital they inherit is tax free and can be spent without any tax consequences. Furthermore, your common-law spouse can gradually reinvest the money in their own ISA.

Passing on ISA savings may not be the most tax efficient route when it comes to leaving money to your children.

Your Children

When you die your ISAs will form part of your estate for inheritance tax purposes (although certain AIM shares are exempt after two years).

Inheritance tax at 40% is payable on assets that exceed the threshold – currently £325,000 but up to £650,000 for married couples. A new additional nil rate band is also available on the family home which will rise to £175,000 by 2020/21 (up to £350,000 for married couples).

If your ISA savings are not subject to inheritance tax your children will effectively inherit a tax-free lump sum, although the money will be inherited outside the ISA tax wrapper.

If your children inherit your pension pot there is usually no inheritance tax payable. They can then withdraw money from it as and when they like. The investments inside the pension will continue to grow tax free.

If you die before age 75 your children can withdraw all the money tax free. If you die after reaching age 75 they will pay income tax on any money they take out.

If your children are working when they inherit your pension savings, there's a good chance they will end up paying 40% income tax on any money they take out, unless they leave the money untouched until they themselves retire (and pay tax at 20% possibly).

In summary, if your estate will not be subject to inheritance tax your children may be better off inheriting your ISAs rather than your pension.

If your estate is subject to inheritance tax they may be better off, pound for pound, inheriting your pension savings – but only if they will pay less than 40% tax when they take the money out.

Are ISAs Still a Good Investment?

In Chapter 14 it was shown that pensions are usually a much better tax shelter than ISAs (although the new Lifetime ISA will be better for some taxpayers). However, there are 17 million ISA savers in Britain and I'm one of them!

What attracts so many people to ISAs is their flexibility. You can withdraw money at any time. Pension investors have to wait until they reach the minimum retirement age of 55 or older.

As with everything in life, a compromise is usually the best solution. There's no harm in using both.

And as we will see in the next two chapters, an ISA may be a great place to park money **before** you invest it in a pension.

Part 4

Postponing & Accelerating Pension Saving

Chapter 16

Basic-Rate Taxpayers: Should They Make Pension Contributions?

Financial advisors usually advise people to start making pension contributions as early as possible. They usually point to the 'magic' of compound interest. Compound interest – earning interest on interest – seems to possess magical powers, making millionaires out of just about anyone who starts early enough.

However, what I think financial advisors often get confused about is saving in a pension with saving *generally*. It's never too early to start saving... but it may be too early to start saving in a pension.

In previous chapters I have shown that higher-rate taxpayers enjoy twice as much tax relief on their pension contributions as basic-rate taxpayers. A higher-rate taxpayer is someone who has taxable income of more than £45,000 in 2017/18 (£43,000 in Scotland).

So the question is, should you delay making pension contributions if you are currently a basic-rate taxpayer but expect to become a higher-rate taxpayer in the future?

More specifically, should you invest your savings somewhere else, for example in a tax-free ISA, and transfer the money into a pension when you will enjoy much more income tax relief?

This is the question we will answer in this chapter.

Are You a Temporary Basic-Rate Taxpayer?

There are lots of reasons why an individual may be a basic-rate taxpayer in one tax year but a higher-rate taxpayer in another tax year.

The most obvious reason is career progression: a graduate earns a lot less income than someone with the same qualifications and

20 years' work experience. You may start your working life as a basic-rate taxpayer and become a higher-rate taxpayer a number of years later.

Many self-employed business owners who are normally higher-rate taxpayers may be basic-rate taxpayers from time to time, either because their incomes fall during tough economic conditions or because they have abnormally high tax-deductible expenditure during any given tax year, for example if they make significant investments in equipment.

Many company directors are also basic-rate taxpayers in some years but higher-rate taxpayers in other years, for example if they pay themselves a small dividend during one tax year and a big dividend during another tax year.

Wealth Warning

There is one group of individuals who should always consider making pension contributions, even if they are only temporary basic-rate taxpayers: company employees who belong to generous workplace pension schemes. For them tax relief is only one of the benefits of making pension contributions. The employer will often match, or more than match, the contribution made by the employee – effectively handing over free cash which no thrifty person would turn down (more on this in Chapter 21).

Case Study – Postponing Pension Contributions

Penny and Isabella are both basic-rate taxpayers but expect to be higher-rate taxpayers in three years' time. Both want to save £3,000 per year but they have different strategies. Penny decides to put her savings in a personal pension straight away because her father has advised her to start saving for retirement as soon as possible. Isabella also wants to save for her retirement but she also wants to maximise her tax relief. She decides to invest in an ISA until she is a higher-rate taxpayer and then transfer the money into a pension.

Who ends up better off?

Table 3
Pension vs ISA
Temporary Basic-Rate Taxpayers

End Year	Pension £	ISA £
1	4,013	3,210
2	8,306	6,645
3	12,900	10,320

We'll assume they both enjoy investment returns of 7% per year (tax-free inside both an ISA and pension). Penny's £3,000 annual investment is topped up with £750 of free cash from the taxman so her gross pension contribution is £3,750. After a year this will have grown to £4,013. After three years she will have £12,900.

Isabella's £3,000 ISA investment will be worth £3,210 after one year. After three years she will have £10,320. The results are summarised in Table 3. For every £1 Penny has in her pension, Isabella has just 80p – the difference is down to the 20% basic-rate tax relief Penny enjoys on her pension contributions.

Becoming Higher-rate Taxpayers

It's the start of the fourth tax year and Isabella knows she will be a higher-rate taxpayer this year. So she decides to take her £10,320 ISA savings and stick them into her pension plan. The taxman will add £2,580 in basic-rate tax relief and, hey presto, she has £12,900 sitting in her pension plan, just like Penny.

However, as a higher-rate taxpayer, Isabella will also receive higher-rate tax relief when she submits her tax return. To calculate this we simply multiply her gross pension contribution by 20%:

£12,900 x 20% = £2,580

In summary, Penny and Isabella have both saved exactly the same amount of money but because Isabella waited until she became a higher-rate taxpayer before making pension contributions she ends up with £2,580 more than Penny.

Maximising the Pension Pot

In the above example Isabella has the same amount of money as Penny in her pension plus a tax refund from HMRC. However, if Isabella would prefer to maximise her pension savings she could do things slightly differently.

What she could do is make a bigger pension contribution – £13,760 instead of just her £10,320 ISA savings. The taxman will top this up with £3,440 to produce a gross pension contribution of £17,200. Isabella won't be out of pocket despite making a bigger contribution because she will also receive a tax refund of £3,440 (£17,200 x 20%) – her higher-rate relief.

This means her total personal investment will simply be the amount she saved up in her ISA:

£13,760 pension contribution *minus* £3,440 tax refund = £10,320

Now look at the size of Isabella's pension pot. She has £17,200 compared with Penny's £12,900 – 33% more money!

33% – The Magic Number

The same 33% increase in pension savings can be enjoyed by anyone who postpones making pension contributions while temporarily a basic-rate taxpayer.

Regardless of whether you postpone for one year, 10 years or any other time period, and regardless of whether you are making big or small pension contributions, the result is exactly the same:

Your pension pot will be 33% bigger

It's a bit like buying a bottle of fine wine and storing it away, instead of drinking it immediately. Good things come to those who wait.

Finally, remember that, although Isabella postpones her pension contributions, she does NOT postpone saving. Note too that she invests in an ISA so that, like Penny, she does not miss out on tax-free growth.

Practical Pointers

- The assumption is that Isabella enjoys the maximum higher-rate tax relief on her £17,200 pension contribution. However, we know from Chapter 3 that Isabella will only enjoy full higher-rate tax relief if she also has at least £17,200 of income taxed at 40%. If she doesn't, she may have to spread her pension contributions over more than one tax year.

- Isabella personally contributes £13,760, which is more than her £10,320 ISA savings. However, when she gets her tax refund back she is not left out of pocket. How do we calculate the number £13,760? Simply divide £10,320 by 0.75 to add on the higher-rate tax relief.

Chapter 17

Higher-Rate Taxpayers: Can They Put Off Pension Saving?

In the previous chapter I showed how basic-rate taxpayers may be better off postponing pension contributions until they become higher-rate taxpayers. What about higher-rate taxpayers – can they also put off making pension contributions?

Be careful about asking a financial advisor this question by the way. It's like giving Superman Kryptonite. They usually advise people to start making pension contributions as soon as possible. However, as I pointed out in the previous chapter, they often confuse the benefits of saving in a pension with the benefits of saving *generally*.

There are lots of reasons why you might not feel like putting money into a pension right now, even though you would receive lots of tax relief. It all revolves around the lengthy jail sentence placed on pension savings – you can't access them until you are age 55 or older.

If you have big financial commitments, for example a mortgage or children's education to pay for many years, you may be very reluctant to tie up your savings in a pension.

You certainly shouldn't be making any pension contributions if you are in imminent danger of losing a big chunk or all of your income, for example if your business is struggling or you are worried about losing your job.

Am I saying it's not necessary to save in these situations? No, I'm a big fan of saving from day one. What I am saying is that you don't necessarily have to save via a pension... not at certain stages of your life at least. It's a fat lot of good having £100,000 in your pension pot if your home's about to be repossessed.

Before making any pension contributions, you should always make sure you have a significant amount of money saved elsewhere to protect against:

- An unforeseen drop in income, and
- Unforeseen expenses

But what about all the tax savings enjoyed by pension savers? If you delay putting money into a pension, won't you lose out? This is one of the great misconceptions about pensions.

As it happens, if you want immediate access to your savings, you don't have to put money into a pension until you are ready.

You will not be one penny worse off than someone who makes pension contributions continually for many years.

I've never heard any pension experts make this crucial point. Maybe it's because advising people to put off making pension contributions is bad for business, a bit like a tobacco company telling you to quit smoking.

Case Study – Postponing Pension Contributions

In Chapter 14 we compared Peter the pension saver with Ian the ISA investor. What we discovered is that pensions are much more powerful than traditional ISAs – you could end up with at least 42% more income from a pension.

However, it is possible that Ian, the ISA investor, will have the last laugh. Let's say he originally started saving into an ISA because he wanted access to his savings. Back then he was worried about losing his job and also had a big mortgage and three children to support. Move forward five years, his career's going well, the mortgage is smaller and the children have all flown the nest.

So he decides to take his ISA savings and stick them into a pension. Is he still worse off than Peter, who started saving in a pension five years earlier?

Table 4
Postponing Pension Contributions
Higher-Rate Taxpayers

End Year	Pension £	ISA £
1	10,700	6,420
2	22,149	13,289
3	34,399	20,640
4	47,507	28,504
5	61,533	36,920

Peter and Ian's savings up to the end of year five are summarised in Table 4. Just to recap, both are higher-rate taxpayers and both personally invest £6,000 per year. Peter enjoys income tax relief so his gross pension contribution is £10,000 per year, compared with Ian's £6,000 ISA investment. They both enjoy tax-free growth of 7% per year. After one year their £10,000 and £6,000 initial investments will be worth £10,700 and £6,420 respectively (explaining the first numbers you see in the table).

After five years Peter has £61,533, compared with Ian's £36,920. Ian now takes his ISA savings and sticks them in a pension. Because he knows he'll get a tax refund (his higher-rate tax relief) he actually makes an investment of £49,226 (£36,920/0.75). The taxman adds £12,307 of basic-rate tax relief and, hey presto, Ian ends up with £61,533 sitting in his pension pot – exactly the same as Peter!

Ian also gets a tax refund of £12,307 (£61,533 x 20%), so his £49,226 pension investment costs him just £36,920 personally – exactly the amount he accumulated in ISAs.

In summary, Peter started saving in a pension from day one, whereas Ian put his savings into an ISA, before transferring the money into a pension five years later. By postponing his pension contributions, Ian was able to access his savings in the event of a financial emergency. Postponing his contributions has not left him out of pocket.

Postponing Pension Contributions – The Dangers

I'm not encouraging anyone to postpone making pension contributions. The point of this exercise is to show that, all things being equal, there is *mathematically* no difference between regular pension contributions and a big catch-up pension contribution. Saving in a pension over many years will not leave you better off.

As with everything, compromise is often the best solution. There's nothing to stop you making some pension contributions now and further catch-up contributions when your personal financial situation is healthier.

There are also some dangers and some very important practical issues when it comes to postponing pension contributions:

Danger # 1 Higher Rate Tax Relief Could Be Scrapped

We discussed this danger in Chapter 5. For many years there have been fears that higher-rate tax relief on pension contributions will be scrapped because it costs the Government so much (apparently around £7 billion per year).

One option would be to give everyone the same flat rate of tax relief (such as 30%). Such a change would be more generous to basic-rate taxpayers but punish higher-rate taxpayers.

Alternatively, higher-rate tax relief could be kept but with the annual allowance reduced from £40,000 to, say, £30,000 or less.

Even if the newly elected Conservative Government makes no changes to pension tax relief, there's nothing to stop a future government making the system less generous. Remember pensions are ultra long-term savings vehicles and your contributions will be made under multiple governments, possibly with widely differing views on tax.

Many higher-rate taxpayers may therefore feel that it is wise not to postpone making pension contributions and make hay while the sun is still shining, i.e. make pension contributions NOW while higher-rate tax relief is still available.

Danger # 2 Loss of Employer Pension Contributions

If you belong to a workplace pension scheme and your employer is matching the contributions you make personally, postponing contributions could prove costly: you will lose a lot of free cash being offered by your employer (see Chapter 21).

Danger # 3 Your Earnings Fall

If your income falls and you are no longer a higher-rate taxpayer when the time comes to make catch-up contributions, you will not enjoy any higher-rate tax relief.

This could happen if you own a business that enters a long tough patch or period of decline. It could also happen to a company employee who suffers redundancy and is unable to find another job that pays well.

Danger # 4 Pension Recycling Rules

If you make larger than normal pension contributions a couple of years before you withdraw tax-free cash from your pension, there is a danger that HMRC will argue that you are recycling your tax-free lump sum.

If the recycling rules are triggered, your tax-free lump sum will be treated as an unauthorised payment, resulting in a tax charge of up to 70% (see Chapter 8).

According to HMRC, the recycling rules will also apply if, instead of funding the pension contribution directly from your tax-free lump sum, you use your available savings to pay the contribution and then use your tax-free lump sum to replenish those savings.

The recycling rules will be triggered if you always intended your tax-free lump sum to be an integral way of paying the increased pension contributions, albeit indirectly.

It's difficult to quantify the risk of triggering the recycling rules but the uncertainty alone is good enough reason to be careful of making bigger than normal pension contributions within a couple of years of withdrawing tax-free cash from your pension.

Practical Issue # 1 Maximising Higher Rate Tax Relief

Ian has to make a gross pension contribution of £61,533 to catch up with Peter. We know from Chapter 3 that to obtain the maximum higher-rate tax relief he must also have at least £61,533 of income taxed at 40%. Most people don't.

The bigger your catch-up contribution, the less likely you are to obtain the maximum higher-rate tax relief. Fortunately, there is a possible solution: Ian could spread his catch-up contributions over several tax years to maximise his higher-rate tax relief. This means he shouldn't leave it too close to retirement to make his catch-up contributions, especially if he has other savings he would like to put into a pension in addition to his ISA savings.

Practical Issue # 2 Exceeding the Annual Allowance

The bigger your catch-up contribution, the more likely you are to exceed the annual allowance (see Chapter 2). The annual allowance was reduced from £50,000 to £40,000 at the start of the 2014/15 tax year and could be reduced further in the years ahead.

Fortunately, it is possible to carry forward any unused annual allowance from the three previous tax years, so a gross pension contribution of up to £160,000 is allowed in 2017/18, provided you have sufficient relevant UK earnings and belonged to a pension scheme in each of those years.

Again, the best practical solution for Ian would probably be to spread his contributions over several tax years.

Practical Issue # 3 Tax Free Growth

Ian is able to catch up with Peter because he also enjoys tax-free investment growth in his ISA. If Ian's savings are taxed, he will end up permanently worse off, even after he puts his savings in a pension.

In summary, it is possible to put off pension saving if you don't want to tie up your money right now... but there are dangers and practical obstacles.

Chapter 18

How to Protect Your Child Benefit

Child benefit is an extremely valuable tax-free gift from the Government to parents. Those who qualify currently receive the following annual payments:

- £1,076.40 for the first child
- £712.40 for each subsequent child

Depending on the number of children, a family can expect to receive the following total child benefit payment:

Children	Total Child Benefit
1	£1,076
2	£1,789
3	£2,501
4	£3,214

plus £712.40 for each additional child

You can keep receiving child benefit until your children are 16 years of age or until age 20 if they are enrolled in 'relevant education' (the likes of GCSEs, A Levels, and NVQs to level 3, but not degree courses).

That's the good news. The bad news is the Government withdraws the benefit where any member of the household has annual income in excess of £50,000.

The withdrawal operates by levying an income tax charge on the highest earner in the household.

How the Child Benefit Charge Works

For every £100 the highest earner's income exceeds £50,000, there is a tax charge equivalent to 1% of the child benefit. So if the highest earner in the household has an income of £51,000, the tax charge is 10% of the child benefit.

For a household with two children this means a tax charge of £178 (£1,789 x 10%, rounded down to the nearest whole pound).

If the highest earner has an income of £55,000, the tax charge is 50% of the child benefit. For a household with two children this means a tax charge of £894.

Once the highest earner's income reaches £60,000, all the child benefit will effectively have been withdrawn.

As an alternative to the income tax charge, the claimant can choose not to receive child benefit.

1970s Style Tax Rates

The child benefit charge creates some truly eye-watering marginal tax rates for some parents with income between £50,000 and £60,000.

For example, let's say the highest earner's taxable income goes up from £50,000 to £51,000.

They will pay £400 more income tax and a 10% child benefit charge – £107 for a household with one child. So the total tax charge on the additional £1,000 is £507 – that's a marginal tax rate of 51%!

And if you think that's bad, take a look at the marginal tax rates suffered by parents with more than one child:

2 Children   58%
3 Children   65%
4 Children   72%

You can add an extra 2% to all of the above tax rates to take account of national insurance, if your income is from employment or self-employment. The marginal tax rates for dividends are different.

Not all Income is Equal

The child benefit charge only applies if your 'adjusted net income' is over £50,000. Adjusted net income includes all income subject to income tax, including income from employment, profits from self employment, pensions and income from property, savings and dividends.

Income from tax-free investments like ISAs is excluded. What this means is that a parent with work-related income of £50,000 and tax-free dividends of £10,000 from an ISA will avoid the child benefit charge completely; someone with the same £50,000 of earned income but £10,000 of rental income will effectively lose all of their child benefit.

This makes investments like shares and bonds (that can be sheltered inside an ISA) potentially far more tax efficient than rental property.

For example, that £10,000 in rental income will produce an income tax bill of £4,000 and a child benefit charge of £1,789 for a family with two children. Total rental income net of all taxes is just £4,211.

The ISA investor ends up with 137% more income!

How Pension Contributions Can Help You Avoid the Child Benefit Charge

One of the simplest ways for almost all taxpayers to avoid the child benefit charge is by making pension contributions. Your adjusted net income is reduced by your gross pension contributions.

In Chapter 17 we looked at the pros and cons of postponing pension contributions. However, those with income in the £50,000-£60,000 bracket are a special case. They should be very wary of postponing making pension contributions if they are subject to the child benefit charge.

In fact, people in this income group should consider *accelerating* their pension contributions, i.e. making bigger contributions now and smaller ones when their incomes rise above £60,000.

The key tax planning point is that you shouldn't necessarily think in terms of avoiding the child benefit charge completely or permanently. It may be possible for some taxpayers (especially those earning just over £50,000) to achieve this best case scenario.

For those with income close to £60,000 (or over £60,000 in some cases) it may be more practical to think in terms of reducing only part of the charge or reducing it in some tax years but not others.

Let's take a look at some of the potential tax savings:

Example
Alan has taxable income of £55,000. His wife earns £30,000 and claims child benefit for three children: £2,501. On the top £5,000 slice of his income, Alan faces a £2,000 income tax bill and a child benefit charge of £1,250 (50%). Alan's £5,000 is reduced to just £1,750.

Let's focus in on that top £5,000 slice of his income and see how he can protect himself from the child benefit charge:

Alan personally contributes £4,000 into his pension. The taxman adds £1,000 of basic-rate tax relief, producing a gross pension contribution of £5,000. When Alan submits his tax return he also receives £1,000 of higher-rate tax relief (£5,000 x 20%).

Furthermore, because Alan's adjusted net income has fallen to £50,000, he escapes the £1,250 child benefit charge.

Alan enjoys a total of £3,250 tax relief on his £5,000 pension contribution, i.e. 65% tax relief.

He ends up with £5,000 in his pension pot instead of £1,750 in after-tax income.

What this example shows is that many parents in the £50,000-£60,000 bracket will enjoy tax relief on their pension contributions of 58% (two children), 65% (three children) or maybe even more, compared with the 40% tax relief enjoyed by most other higher-rate taxpayers.

Hence it's not just basic-rate taxpayers who should consider postponing pension contributions until their incomes rise (see Chapter 16). Higher-rate taxpayers with income over £45,000 (£43,000 in Scotland) but under £50,000 may wish to consider postponing pension contributions if they expect to be in the £50,000-£60,000 income bracket in the near future and subject to the child benefit charge.

Similarly, where one spouse or partner is in the £50,000-£60,000 income bracket, and the other has a smaller income, it may be worth getting the higher earner to make most of the family's pension contributions, even for just one or two tax years.

Example

Chris and Maria are both higher-rate taxpayers earning £60,000 and £50,000 respectively. They receive child benefit for two children: £1,789. In the past they've each made pension contributions of £5,000.

In 2017/18 the couple decide that Maria should stop her pension contributions and Chris should increase his by £5,000 to £10,000. By making an additional £5,000 pension contribution Chris will avoid an additional 50% child benefit charge, saving the couple £894.

Bigger than Normal Pension Contributions

Those in the £50,000-£60,000 income bracket should consider making bigger than normal pension contributions, in particular if they expect their income to rise above £60,000 in the future or if their children are approaching the age where child benefit will be withdrawn.

Example

Gordon has taxable income of £60,000 in 2017/18. His wife earns £30,000 and claims child benefit for two children: £1,789. On the top £10,000 slice of his income, Gordon faces a 58% tax charge: £4,000 income tax and a £1,789 child benefit charge.

Gordon wouldn't normally make a gross pension contribution of more than £5,000 but decides to double his contribution for the current tax year so that he can take advantage of the 58% tax relief available (two children).

He could then suspend making any pension contributions in 2018/19, for example if his income rises from £60,000 to £65,000. A £5,000 pension contribution in 2018/19 would attract just 40% tax relief, compared with the 58% available in 2017/18.

Much Bigger than Normal Pension Contributions

Even those with income *over* £60,000 can enjoy above average levels of tax relief by making bigger than normal pension contributions.

Example
Colin has taxable income of £65,000 in 2017/18. His wife earns £30,000 and receives child benefit for three children: £2,501. On the top £15,000 slice of his income, Colin faces an £8,501 tax charge: £6,000 income tax and a £2,501 child benefit charge.

If Colin makes a gross pension contribution of £5,000 he will enjoy 40% tax relief, just like most other higher-rate taxpayers. He will not avoid any of the child benefit charge because his adjusted net income will not fall below £60,000.

Fortunately his aunt Doris left him some money so Colin decides to make a much bigger than normal £15,000 gross pension contribution in 2017/18 and then stop making contributions for a year or two.

Colin's pension contribution attracts £6,000 income tax relief and, by reducing his adjusted net income to £50,000, allows him to entirely avoid the £2,501 child benefit charge. The total tax relief is £8,501 or 57% of his gross pension contribution.

Obviously the higher your income the bigger the pension contribution you have to make to get your income below £60,000 and ultimately down to £50,000. However, for some individuals, including those with income well over £60,000, the tax relief may make it worthwhile

The Self-Employed

The taxable income of self-employed individuals (sole traders etc) tends to fluctuate more than that of salaried employees and even company owners.

A self-employed individual's taxable income is essentially the pre-tax profits of the business. These will vary from year to year if business conditions improve or decline or if the business owner alters the level of tax deductible spending (e.g. by making investments in tax deductible equipment or vehicles).

As a result some self-employed business owners, who are also parents of qualifying children, may find themselves in the £50,000-£60,000 income bracket in some tax years but not others.

Where possible they should consider always making pension contributions in those '£50,000-£60,000' tax years, possibly contributions that are bigger than normal.

Both Partners Earn £50,000-£60,000

Where both income earners in the household are in the £50,000-£60,000 bracket, the most tax-efficient strategy is to *equalise* their adjusted net incomes.

Example
Alistair earns £58,000, his wife Wilma earns £55,000. The couple want to make a £5,000 gross pension contribution in 2017/18. If Alistair makes the entire contribution this will take his adjusted net income to £53,000. Wilma will then become the household's highest earner with £55,000, resulting in a 50% child benefit charge.

The best solution may be for Alistair to make a £4,000 gross pension contribution, with Wilma making a £1,000 gross contribution. They will both then have adjusted net income of £54,000 and an additional 10% of their child benefit will be retained.

Other Considerations & Drawbacks

To maximise the tax relief on pension contributions it may be necessary to postpone or bring forward contributions or have one household member make bigger contributions than another.

Actions like these may have other consequences that need to be considered. For example, the second member of the household may not be happy about the highest earner accumulating all the retirement savings!

Postponing pension contributions may not be a good idea if this means you forfeit contributions from your employer (see Chapter 21) or if higher-rate tax relief is eventually abolished (see Chapter 5).

Chapter 19

Higher Income Earners

Income between £100,000 and £123,000

Once your income exceeds £100,000 your income tax personal allowance is gradually taken away. It is reduced by £1 for every £2 you earn above £100,000.

For example, if your income is £110,000 your personal allowance will be reduced by £5,000.

The income tax personal allowance for the 2017/18 tax year is £11,500. So once your income reaches £123,000 you will have no personal allowance at all.

This is a real tax sting for those earning over £100,000. The personal allowance currently saves you £4,600 in tax if you are a higher-rate taxpayer.

Paying Tax at 60%

The effect of having your personal allowance taken away is that anyone earning between £100,000 and £123,000 faces a hefty marginal income tax rate of 60%.

For example, someone who earns £100,000 and receives an extra £10,000 will pay 40% tax on the extra income – £4,000.

They'll also have their personal allowance reduced by £5,000, which means they'll have to pay an extra £2,000 in tax (£5,000 x 40%). Total tax on extra income: £6,000 which is 60%!

Saving Tax at 60%

The flipside of this is that anyone in this income bracket who makes pension contributions can currently enjoy 60% tax relief.

Your personal allowance is reduced if your 'adjusted net income' is more than £100,000. When calculating your adjusted net income you usually deduct any pension contributions you have made.

For example, let's say you have taxable income of £110,000 and invest £8,000 in a pension. For starters you will receive a £2,000 top up from the taxman (your basic-rate tax relief), resulting in a gross pension contribution of £10,000. You'll also receive higher-rate tax relief of £2,000 (£10,000 x 20%).

In addition, by making a gross pension of £10,000 your 'adjusted net income' will be reduced from £110,000 to £100,000, so none of your personal allowance will be taken away. Additional tax saving: £2,000 (£5,000 x 40%).

In summary, your £10,000 pension contribution produces £6,000 of tax savings – a total of 60% tax relief!

Income over £123,000

Once your income rises above £123,000 your marginal income tax rate falls back to 40%. However, making quite big pension contributions can still be attractive because you may still get 60% tax relief on some of the money you put away.

For example, let's say you have taxable income of £130,000 and put £24,000 into a pension. Like anyone else you will receive £6,000 basic-rate tax relief, resulting in a gross pension contribution of £30,000. And like any other higher-rate taxpayer you will receive an additional £6,000 of higher-rate relief (£30,000 x 20%).

In addition, your £30,000 gross pension contribution will reduce your adjusted net income from £130,000 to £100,000, so none of your personal allowance will be taken away. Additional tax saving: £4,600 (£11,500 x 40%).

In summary, your £30,000 gross pension contribution produces £16,600 of tax savings – a total of 55% tax relief!

In fact, anyone with taxable income up to £146,000 will enjoy *at least* 50% tax relief by making a gross pension contribution that's big enough to take their adjusted net income back down to £100,000.

For example, someone with taxable income of £146,000 would need to make a gross pension contribution of £46,000 to take their adjusted net income back down to £100,000 and enjoy exactly 50% tax relief.

Although the tax relief is attractive, that's a big pension contribution, so in practice this strategy may appeal most to those whose income is only slightly higher than the £123,000 threshold.

Furthermore, pension contributions in excess of £40,000 will exceed the annual allowance and are only possible if you have unused annual allowance from the three previous tax years.

Income over £150,000

When your income rises above £150,000 you become an additional-rate taxpayer and start paying tax at 45% on most types of income. The flipside is you can enjoy 45% tax relief on your pension contributions.

However, additional-rate taxpayers face greater restrictions to their pension contributions than other taxpayers. From 6 April 2016 the annual allowance (normally £40,000) is reduced if your "adjusted income" exceeds £150,000.

Broadly speaking, your adjusted income is your total taxable income plus any pension contributions made by your employer.

The inclusion of employer pension contributions means you cannot prevent your annual allowance being reduced by taking a smaller salary in exchange for higher pension contributions from your employer.

You must also add back any contributions you've made to an occupational pension scheme under a net pay arrangement (where employee contributions are deducted by the employer before calculating tax under PAYE).

When calculating your adjusted income you can also deduct certain reliefs listed in Section 24 of the Income Tax Act 2007.

If your adjusted income exceeds £150,000, your annual allowance will be gradually reduced from £40,000 to £10,000. £1 of allowance will be lost for every additional £2 of income:

Adjusted Income	Annual allowance
£150,000	£40,000
£160,000	£35,000
£170,000	£30,000
£180,000	£25,000
£190,000	£20,000
£200,000	£15,000
£210,000+	£10,000

Once your adjusted income reaches £210,000 there will be no further reductions below £10,000 in your annual allowance.

As long as your contributions do not exceed the reduced annual allowance you will still receive full tax relief, typically at 45%.

Clearly the new rules do not just affect those with income over £150,000. For example, someone with a salary of £120,000 and a pension contribution of £40,000 from their employer will have adjusted income of £160,000 and will have their annual allowance reduced to £35,000 and could therefore end up paying the annual allowance charge.

Threshold Income

Your annual allowance will not be reduced if your "threshold income" is £110,000 or less.

Your threshold income is, broadly speaking, your total taxable income less any pension contributions you have made personally (you deduct the gross value of your pension contributions if they're made under the relief at source method).

Employer pension contributions are ignored when calculating threshold income. But you must add back any salary sacrificed in exchange for employer pension contributions this year if the arrangement started on or after 9 July 2015.

Broadly speaking, adjusted income includes all pension contributions (including employer contributions) while threshold income excludes pension contributions.

When calculating your threshold income you can also deduct the reliefs listed in Section 24 of the Income Tax Act 2007.

Example

Mario is a company owner with taxable income of £100,000. He gets his company to make a £60,000 contribution into his pension (carrying forward unused annual allowance). His adjusted income is £160,000 but his threshold income is £100,000, so his annual allowance is not reduced.

Anti-Avoidance Rules

Measures have been put in place to prevent you entering into an arrangement which involves reducing either your adjusted or threshold income and redressing the reduction in a different tax year.

The anti-avoidance provisions apply when it is reasonable to assume that the main purpose, or one of the main purposes of the arrangement, is to increase your annual allowance.

If the anti-avoidance provisions apply, then the relevant arrangement will be ignored for the purposes of calculating the tapered annual allowance.

The Tapered Annual Allowance and Carry Forward

Fortunately, all is not lost if your pension contributions exceed your tapered annual allowance for the year. Those affected by the tapered annual allowance can still carry forward any unused annual allowance from the three previous tax years.

Carry forward could therefore act as a lifeline for those whose pension contributions accidentally exceed the tapered annual allowance in any given year.

For example, if your annual allowance last year (2016/17) was reduced from £40,000 to £30,000 and you made a £20,000 pension contribution, you will have £10,000 left to carry forward to the current year (£30,000 - £20,000).

The taper did not apply before 2016/17 so it is possible you will have up to £40,000 of unused annual allowance from each of the 2014/15 and 2015/16 tax years to use this year.

Calculating the Tapered Annual Allowance in Practice

Some individuals will find it fairly easy to calculate their adjusted and threshold income, for example many salaried employees and company owners.

Company owners should also find it relatively easy to reduce the amount of income they extract from their companies in order to stay below the thresholds and make full use of the maximum £40,000 annual allowance.

However, problems may arise when the individual has other income that is less predictable, for example rental income from properties. If you have income from other sources you may not know precisely how much taxable income you have earned (and thus your tapered annual allowance) until *after* the tax year has ended. By then it will be too late to make pension contributions.

Those who wish to benefit from pension contributions and think they may be affected by the tapered annual allowance may therefore need to estimate their taxable income before pension contributions are made.

Planning under the Tapered Annual Allowance

Some high income earners may be comfortable with a reduced annual allowance. For example, a sole trader with profits of £170,000 who makes regular pension contributions of £20,000 per year may be quite happy with an annual allowance of £30,000.

However, if they expect their income to increase, resulting in further reductions in their annual allowance, it may be desirable for them to make bigger pension contributions now while they can, i.e. to contribute £30,000 now instead of £20,000.

Some individuals with income *below* £150,000 may also wish to speed up their pension contributions at present if they expect to be earning well over £150,000 in a few years time.

Even though these additional contributions may only enjoy 40% tax relief, 40% tax relief on a £40,000 pension contribution is still better than 45% tax relief on a £10,000 pension contribution!

It may also be possible to mitigate the damage caused by the reduced annual allowance by getting your spouse to make bigger pension contributions, even if they only attract 40% tax relief.

Example
Miriam is a sole trader with profits of £250,000 and her husband Nick earns £85,000. During the current tax year Miriam would like to make a pension contribution of £40,000 but is restricted to £10,000. Nick normally makes pension contributions of £10,000 per year.

The couple therefore decide to swap the amounts they contribute: Nick contributes £40,000 per year (using the couple's shared resources) and Miriam contributes £10,000.

Nick's additional pension contribution of £30,000 will only attract 40% tax relief, compared with Miriam's 45%, however the total loss of tax relief is just £1,500 (£30,000 x 5%).

For this strategy to work it is essential that Nick has sufficient income taxed at 40% so that all of the additional contribution attracts higher-rate tax relief (see Chapter 3).

It may also be essential that Nick's higher contributions do not result in him building such a big pension pot that his withdrawals, when he eventually retires, are taxed at 40% instead of 20%.

Part 5

Employees

Chapter 20

Auto-Enrolment: The Advent of Compulsory Pensions

"Currently 14 million people get no contribution from their employer towards a pension."

Former Secretary of State for Work and Pensions, Yvette Cooper, January 2010

To address this problem, compulsory workplace pensions have been phased in over the last few years. Known as 'auto enrolment' it forces all employers to enrol nearly all their staff into a workplace pension by February 2018.

Exemptions

Only employees earning more than £10,000 and aged from 22 to state pension age need to be *automatically* enrolled into a pension. However, some older and younger employees and those who earn less than £10,000 also have workplace pension rights:

- If an employee earns less than £5,876 they don't need to be automatically enrolled but the employer has to give them access to a pension if they request it and if they are aged between 16 and 74. However, the employer is not required to contribute.

- If an employee earns between £5,876 and £10,000 and their age is between 16 and 74 they don't need to be automatically enrolled but do have the right to opt in. If they do decide to join the pension scheme the employer will have to contribute as well.

- If an employee earns more than £10,000 but is aged 16-21 or between state pension age and 74 they don't need to be automatically enrolled but do have the right to opt in. If they do decide to join the pension scheme the employer will have to contribute as well.

Company Directors

According to the Pension Regulator a company does not have any automatic-enrolment duties when:

- It has just one director, with no other staff

- It has a number of directors, none of whom has an employment contract, with no other staff

- It has a number of directors, only one of whom has an employment contract, with no other staff

A contract of employment does not have to be in writing. However, according to the Pension Regulator, if there is no written contract of employment, or other evidence of an intention to create an employer/worker relationship between the company and the director, it will not argue that an employment contract exists.

If a director does not have an employment contract they are always exempt from automatic enrolment.

If a director has a contract of employment and there are other people working for the company with an employment contract, they are not exempt.

Depending on their age and earnings, they may qualify for automatic enrolment but the company can decide whether to automatically enrol them into a pension.

However, the director has the right to join a pension scheme at any time and the company cannot refuse to enrol them (although in practice this problem will not arise in most owner-managed companies).

If the company decides not to enrol any employed director who is eligible for automatic enrolment, and it has no other eligible staff, it does not need to set up a pension scheme.

However, it will still need to make a 'declaration of compliance'.

Table 5
Auto-Enrolment: Minimum Contributions

	Employer pays	Total required	Employee could pay
Employer's staging date to 5 April 2018	1%	2%	1%
6 April 2018 to 5 April 2019	2%	5%	3%
From 6 April 2019	3%	8%	5%

The Contributions

Employers are forced to make a minimum pension contribution and, in practice, so too are most employees.

Generally speaking, contributions are a percentage of 'qualifying earnings'. The minimum contribution will be increased gradually until April 2019.

Contributions start at 2% with at least 1% coming from the employer. From 6 April 2019 onwards the total minimum contribution will be 8%, with at least 3% coming from the employer.

The minimum contributions are summarised in Table 5.

The total minimum contribution can be paid by the employer but in practice many small firms will probably insist that the employee makes up the required balance.

This means that from 6 April 2019 onwards many employees will be forced to contribute 5% to a pension if they want to benefit from a 3% contribution from their employer.

Employees' contributions will enjoy tax relief as normal, which means 4% will come from them personally and the extra 1% will be added by the taxman in the form of basic-rate tax relief.

Qualifying Earnings

The minimum contributions are generally not based on the employee's total earnings but rather on a band of earnings.

The lower and upper thresholds for 2017/18 are £5,876 and £45,000 respectively. What this means is that pension contributions are typically based on earnings of up to £39,124 (£45,000 - £5,876).

For example, someone with employment income of £50,000 will have their pension contributions based on earnings of £39,124. Someone with employment income of £20,000 will have their pension contributions based on earnings of £14,124 (£20,000 - £5,876).

Opting out

Employees will be automatically enrolled but can opt out if they wish by completing an opt-out notice. Employers are, however, required to automatically re-enrol eligible employees back into the workplace pension scheme roughly every three years.

No doubt some employees, especially younger employees, will prefer to opt out if they are compelled by their employers to make a pension contribution of up to 5%.

How Valuable is Auto Enrolment?

The answer to this question probably depends on whether you are an employee or employer.

Many small business owners cannot afford to save for their own retirement, let alone those of their entire workforce!

And this, perhaps, is the crucial point. If your employer has been dragged kicking and screaming into a system of compulsory pensions, you may end up being paid less to cover the cost. For example, future pay increases or other employment benefits may be reduced. This is basic economics.

Even an 8% pension contribution is not big enough to solve most people's retirement saving problem, especially since it will typically be based on a small band of the employee's earnings.

For example, let's say you currently earn £50,000 and you and your employer make a combined 8% pension contribution for 20 years (based on the £39,124 band of qualifying earnings), with all amounts increased to take account of inflation.

After 20 years the pension pot will be worth around £130,000, if the investments in the fund grow by, say, 5% per year. That's a tidy sum BUT insignificant in terms of providing you with a meaningful retirement income.

In 20 years' time your salary will have grown to around £73,000, so the money paid into your pension pot will be worth less than two years' salary – not exactly enough for a golden retirement!

This does not mean that you should opt out of auto-enrolment. That would mean forfeiting the pension contribution your employer makes, which could arguably be regarded as free money.

What it does mean is that those who are making the minimum pension contribution under auto enrolment will almost certainly need to build additional retirement savings, either using pensions or other savings products.

Chapter 21

Free Cash from Employers

As we know from the previous chapter, many individuals enjoy more than just tax relief on their pension contributions. They also receive free money from their employers.

Many company pension schemes offer far more generous employer contributions than those required under the auto-enrolment rules. Some employees receive employer contributions totalling 5%-10% of their salary, provided they contribute a similar amount.

With the help of employer pension contributions, you may be able to save twice as quickly as you could on your own. Sometimes employers will double what you put in. For example, in one pension scheme I know about, the company puts in 12% if the employee puts in 6%.

Many employees recognize that giving up any of this free money (by not contributing at all or not contributing enough) is tantamount to looking a gift horse in the mouth.

I remember listening on the radio to a woman describe how she and her husband were trying to cut out every single bit of frivolous spending so that they could contribute as much as possible to her husband's workplace pension scheme, thereby enjoying a hefty matching contribution from the employer.

She described it as "austerity today for prosperity tomorrow".

Not everyone has been as financially prudent as this couple. According to Standard Life, in 2011 employers were offering a contribution to around 10 million employees but around 4.5 million did not sign up to their employer's pension scheme.

These employees were missing out on a total of nearly £6 billion per year of free money!

Not surprisingly in the past it has been younger employees who have contributed the least to pensions. According to the

Department for Work and Pensions, in 2011 only 15% of employees aged 16-24 participated in workplace pension schemes, whereas pension participation was 58% in the 45-54 age group.

Millions more people now belong to a workplace pension thanks to the introduction of compulsory pensions (see Chapter 20) BUT some employees (e.g. younger employees) may opt out.

I'm not in the business of criticising the savings habits of others, especially those who have children to support. Many families have very little income left after paying extortionate amounts of income tax, national insurance and VAT and after paying down debts like student loans and home mortgages.

Nevertheless, if there is ever a good time to contribute to a pension it's when your employer is offering you money on a plate.

Example

Douglas is an employee with a salary of £50,000 per year. Let's say his employer offers to make a 5% pension contribution, with Douglas contributing 5% personally.

If Douglas decides to opt out of his workplace pension scheme, he will have additional income of £2,500 (£50,000 x 5%). After paying income tax he will be left with £1,500.

Alternatively, if Douglas decides to join his workplace pension scheme he will end up with £5,000 sitting in his pension (£2,500 contributed personally and £2,500 from his employer).

Douglas has to decide whether £1,500 of income today is more valuable than £5,000 tucked away until he retires.

This is just a snapshot from a single year. Douglas will lose £3,500 (£5,000 - £1,500) every year he is not a member of his employer's pension scheme. Furthermore, he will also lose the tax-free growth on that money. If a 25-year-old decides to forego a pension contribution from his employer he will lose possibly 40 years of tax-free compound growth. On next year's foregone contribution he will lose 39 years of tax-free growth... and so on.

So how much do you stand to lose over the long term by not receiving pension contributions from your employer?

Example continued

Let's say Douglas opts out of his workplace pension scheme for five years and therefore loses out on five years of employer contributions (at 5% of his salary).

We'll assume his salary increases by 3% per year, which means the contributions from his employer will also grow by 3% per year. We'll also assume the money in his pension grows by 7% per year tax free.

Douglas loses out on the following employer contributions over the five-year period: £2,500, £2,575, £2,652, £2,732 and £2,814. When you add tax-free compound growth at 7% per year, the total value of the employer pension contributions after five years is £16,269.

However, that's not the end of the story. Depending on how far away Douglas is from retirement he could lose out on tax-free growth on this money for possibly another 10, 20, 30 or even 40 years. For example, those five years' worth of contributions will be worth £22,818 after 10 years, £44,887 after 20 years, £88,300 after 30 years and £173,699 after 40 years.

Remember, all we are looking at here are the contributions that would be made by Douglas's employer (the 'free money'). We are ignoring the contributions that he would make personally and on which he would enjoy full income tax relief.

The top half of Table 6 shows exactly the same thing for a range of different starting salaries. In each case we assume the salary grows by 3% per year, the employer makes a 5% pension contribution for five years and the money grows by 7% per year tax free.

For example, if your salary is £30,000 now and you lose out on five years' worth of employer contributions and an additional 15 years of tax-free growth on that money, the total loss to your pension pot after 20 years will be £26,932.

The second half of the table shows exactly the same thing except this time we assume the employee is not a member of the workplace pension scheme for 10 years. For example, if your salary is £30,000 now and you lose out on 10 years' worth of employer contributions and an additional 10 years of tax-free growth on that money, the total loss to your pension pot after 20 years will be £49,193.

Table 6
5% Employer Pension Contribution
Long-term Value

Employer Contributions for 5 Years
Value after...

Starting Salary £	10 Years £	20 Years £	30 Years £	40 Years £
20,000	9127	17,955	35,320	69,480
30,000	13,691	26,932	52,980	104,220
40,000	18,255	35,910	70,640	138,959
50,000	22,818	44,887	88,300	173,699
60,000	27,382	53,865	105,960	208,439
70,000	31,946	62,842	123,620	243,179
80,000	36,509	71,820	141,280	277,919
90,000	41,073	80,797	158,940	312,659
100,000	45,637	89,774	176,600	347,399

Employer Contributions for 10 Years
Value after...

Starting Salary £	10 Years £	20 Years £	30 Years £	40 Years £
20,000	16,672	32,795	64,514	126,908
30,000	25,007	49,193	96,770	190,362
40,000	33,343	65,591	129,027	253,816
50,000	41,679	81,989	161,284	317,270
60,000	50,015	98,386	193,541	380,724
70,000	58,350	114,784	225,798	444,178
80,000	66,686	131,182	258,054	507,632
90,000	75,022	147,579	290,311	571,086
100,000	83,358	163,977	322,568	634,540

Different Employer Pension Contributions

Different employers pay different amounts into their employees' pensions.

To find out how much a bigger or smaller employer contribution is worth all you have to do is scale the numbers in Table 6 up or down.

For example, if the employer offers a 10% contribution you simply double the numbers. In this case Douglas, with a starting salary of £50,000 and no contributions for five years, will have lost £89,774 after 20 years (£44,887 x 2).

If the employer offers an 8% contribution you multiply the numbers by 1.6 (found by dividing 8 by 5).

If the employer offers a 3% contribution you multiply the numbers by 0.6 (found by dividing 3 by 5).

... and so on.

Putting Things in Perspective

The numbers in the table are quite large and imply that, by not belonging to a workplace pension scheme, and not receiving pension contributions from your employer, you may be losing a lot of free money.

However, it's important to put the figures in perspective. Let's say Douglas is 35 years old and 30 years away from retirement. By not receiving employer pension contributions for five years, his pension pot will have lost £88,300 of free money after 30 years.

However, by that time his salary will have grown to £117,828 (growing at just 3% per year). What this means is that not contributing to his employer's pension for five years has cost him around nine months' salary.

Is this a price worth paying? Only Douglas can answer that.

And what if Douglas is a high flier and his pay increases by more than inflation, as he climbs the corporate ladder?

If we assume his salary grows by 7% per year we find that after 30 years he is sitting on a salary of £355,713. And his pension pot will have lost out on £95,153 worth of employer contributions.

In total Douglas will have lost just over three months' pay by not receiving pension contributions from his employer for five years.

Personally, I am of the opinion that anyone offered free cash by their employer should grasp the opportunity with open arms.

BUT...

If you do not belong to your workplace pension scheme for just a few years, this may not have a significant effect on your income in retirement IF you expect your salary to grow rapidly, resulting in bigger employer pension contributions in later years.

Part 6

Salary Sacrifice Pensions

Chapter 22

Introduction to Salary Sacrifice Pensions

How would you like to increase your pension contributions by up to 34%, with the taxman footing the entire bill? It seems too good to be true but this result can be achieved if you stop making pension contributions *personally* and get your employer to make them all for you.

This set-up is known as salary sacrifice (also salary exchange or 'smart pensions') and is used by some of the country's biggest companies, universities and other organisations, including BT, Tesco and the BBC.

In my opinion, a salary sacrifice pension is the best tax-saving opportunity available to regular salaried employees.

So how does it work? Salary sacrifice is all about saving *national insurance*, on top of the income tax relief you already receive when you make pension contributions.

Most people only enjoy income tax relief when they contribute to a pension. The income tax relief is attractive but it's not the maximum amount of tax relief available. When an employee contributes personally to a pension plan there is no refund of all the national insurance paid by both the employee and the employer. As much as £258 of national insurance is paid by the employee and employer on £1,000 of salary.

With salary sacrifice arrangements, it is possible to put a stop to these national insurance payments because your employer makes your pension contributions for you.

Pension contributions paid by employers are exempt from national insurance.

The national insurance savings can then be added to your pension pot.

Sacrificing Salary, Not Income

Because the employer has to pay the employee's pension contributions, the employee in return has to sacrifice some salary.

However, it's important to stress that the employee's net take-home pay does not fall – it remains exactly the same.

With salary sacrifice there are no losers: Both the employee and employer can save money. The only loser is the taxman!

Clamp Down on Salary Sacrifice

The Government has been concerned about the amount of money lost from salary sacrifice schemes so, from 6 April 2017, the income tax and employer's national insurance advantages of some salary sacrifice schemes is being removed.

However, employer pension contributions, employer-provided pensions advice, employer-supported childcare, cycle to work schemes and ultra low emission cars will not be affected and will continue to benefit from income tax and national insurance relief.

Company Pension Scheme Not Required

In theory salary sacrifice works with almost all pension plans including:

- Self-invested personal pensions (SIPPs)
- Personal pensions (group and individual plans)
- Stakeholder pensions (group and individual plans)
- Occupational pension schemes

The main consideration for salary sacrifice purposes is that the plan must be able to accept employer contributions. Many SIPP providers have special forms for this purpose.

However, if a salary sacrifice pension arrangement is used by your employer in conjunction with his auto-enrolment duties, it's essential the pension plan is a "qualifying scheme" for auto-enrolment purposes.

The pension provider will be able to tell you if the scheme is qualifying or not.

Salary sacrifice can be used by most employees. However, sole traders and other self-employed individuals cannot use salary sacrifice because there is no employer to make pension contributions on their behalf.

There has to be an employer/employee relationship for a salary sacrifice arrangement to be successful.

Chapter 23

Income Tax & National Insurance: A Five-Minute Primer

There are several examples in the chapters that follow that use income tax and national insurance rates and allowances. In this chapter I'm going to briefly explain how income tax and national insurance are calculated for the average salary-earning employee. This should make the examples easier to understand (and slightly less painful!).

Calculating Income Tax

For the 2017/18 tax year, which started on 6 April 2017, most employees pay income tax as follows:

- 0%   on the first   £11,500   Personal allowance
- 20% on the next   £33,500   Basic-rate band
- 40% above   £45,000   Higher-rate threshold

If you earn more than £45,000 you are a higher-rate taxpayer; if you earn less you are a basic-rate taxpayer.

If you are a Scottish taxpayer the basic-rate band is £31,500 and so you will be a higher-rate taxpayer if you earn more than £43,000. The examples that follow are based on the rates applying in the rest of the UK.

Example – Basic-Rate Taxpayer

John earns a salary of £25,000. His income tax for 2017/18 can be calculated as follows:

- *0% on the first £11,500 = £0*
- *20% on the next £13,500 = £2,700*

Total income tax bill: £2,700

Example – Higher-Rate Taxpayer

Jane earns a salary of £60,000. Her income tax for 2017/18 can be calculated as follows:

- *0% on the first £11,500 = £0*
- *20% on the next £33,500 = £6,700*
- *40% on the final £15,000 = £6,000*

Total income tax bill: £12,700

Income above £100,000 and £150,000

When your income exceeds £100,000 your tax-free personal allowance is gradually withdrawn and when your income exceeds £150,000 you also start paying tax at 45%.

Calculating National Insurance

For the 2017/18 tax year employees pay national insurance as follows:

- 0%   on the first   £8,164   Primary threshold
- 12%   on the next   £36,836
- 2%   above   £45,000   Upper earnings limit

Employers generally pay 13.8% national insurance on every single pound the employee earns over £8,164. There is no cap.

You probably don't lose much sleep over your employer's national insurance bill. However, employer's national insurance is a tax on YOUR income. If it didn't exist your employer would be able to pay you a higher salary.

Here are John and Jane's national insurance calculations:

Example – Basic-Rate Taxpayer

John earns a salary of £25,000. His national insurance for 2017/18 can be calculated as follows:

- *0%   on the first   £8,164   = £0*
- *12%   on the next   £16,836 = £2,020*

John's national insurance bill: £2,020

John's employer pays national insurance on John's salary as follows:

- *0%   on the first   £8,164   = £0*
- *13.8% on the next   £16,836 = £2,323*

John's employer's national insurance bill: £2,323

Example – Higher-Rate Taxpayer

Jane earns a salary of £60,000. Her national insurance for 2017/18 can be calculated as follows:

- *0%   on the first   £8,164   = £0*
- *12%   on the next   £36,836 = £4,420*
- *2%   on the final   £15,000 = £300*

Jane's national insurance bill: £4,720

Her employer's national insurance is:

- *0%   on the first   £8,164   = £0*
- *13.8% on the next   £51,836 = £7,153*

Jane's employer's national insurance bill: £7,153

Tax Bills Combined

John and Jane's tax bills can be summarised as follows:

John – Basic-rate Taxpayer – £25,000

	£
Income tax	2,700
Employee's national insurance	2,020
Employer's national insurance	2,323
Total taxes	**7,043**

Jane – Higher-rate Taxpayer – £60,000

	£
Income tax	12,700
Employee's national insurance	4,720
Employer's national insurance	7,153
Total taxes	**24,573**

When you include employer's national insurance it's startling how much tax is paid even by those on relatively modest incomes. Direct taxes on John's income come to 28%.

Jane's £60,000 salary is not low by any standards but you wouldn't describe her as a high income earner either. Nevertheless an amount equivalent to 41% of her salary is paid in direct taxes on her income.

Chapter 24

Salary Sacrifice Case Study: Basic-Rate Taxpayer

Introduction

We are going to follow the same John from the previous chapter and show how his own pension contributions can be increased by 34% with a salary sacrifice pension.

Remember John earns £25,000 and is a basic-rate taxpayer. Basic-rate taxpayers pay 20% income tax and 12% national insurance.

John's Retirement Savings

John pays income tax of £2,700 and national insurance of £2,020 on his £25,000 salary.

Let's say he also personally contributes £1,000 into his employer's pension scheme.

His employer pays the amount to the pension scheme provider who in turn reclaims £250 of basic-rate tax relief from HMRC and credits this to John's pension pot, bringing his total pension contribution to £1,250.

(The assumption here is that the pension scheme uses the 'relief at source' method rather than the 'net pay' method – see Chapter 2.)

The company John works for also makes an employer contribution into his pension plan. Although this is welcome, we will ignore this contribution and focus on John's own contributions.

After deducting his taxes and pension contribution he is left with a disposable income of £19,280.

Saving National Insurance

This is not a bad outcome but John can do much better. So far he has enjoyed full *income tax* relief on his pension contributions. However, income tax is not the only tax John pays. He also pays 12% national insurance on a significant chunk of his salary and his employer pays 13.8%.

Unfortunately, there is no national insurance relief for pension contributions made personally by employees like John. However, there is full national insurance relief for pension contributions made by employers.

John and his employer therefore agree that John will stop contributing personally to the pension scheme and his employer will make all the contributions for him. In return, John agrees to sacrifice some salary.

John's Salary Sacrifice

John sacrifices £1,470, which takes his salary from £25,000 to £23,530 (I explain why he sacrifices this amount later).

After deducting income tax and national insurance on £23,530 he is still left with £19,280 – the exact amount of disposable income he had before.

John's employer pays the £1,470 of sacrificed salary directly into John's pension plan.

His employer also contributes an additional £203, representing the employer's national insurance saving: £1,470 x 13.8% = £203. The amount going into John's pension pot now is £1,673 (plus his employer's original pre-salary sacrifice contribution).

In summary, John still has £19,280 of take-home pay, just as before, but his pension contribution has increased from £1,250 to £1,673 – an increase of 34%.

He is now saving 20% income tax, 12% employee's national insurance and 13.8% employer's national insurance on the money paid into his pension plan. A summary of the number crunching is contained on the next page.

John's Take Home Pay Stays the Same

	Before Salary Sacrifice	After Salary Sacrifice
	£	£
Salary	25,000	23,530
Less:		
Income tax	2,700	2,406
National insurance	2,020	1,844
Pension contribution	1,000	0
Disposable income	**19,280**	**19,280**

... But His Pension Contribution Increases By 34%

	Before Salary Sacrifice	After Salary Sacrifice
	£	£
Employee contribution	1,000	-
Taxman's top up	250	-
Extra employer contribution	-	1,470
Employer's NI saving	-	203
Total	**1,250**	**1,673**

34% –The Magic Number!

Although this is just a one-year snapshot, what we can deduce from this simple example is that basic-rate taxpayers who use salary sacrifice can boost their pension contributions by 34%.

This means salary sacrifice could have a BIG impact on the amount of money you are able to save for retirement.

For example, if you would expect your own pension contributions to eventually grow in value to £100,000 without salary sacrifice, then you can expect them to grow to £134,000 with salary sacrifice.

If you would expect your own pension contributions to grow in value to £200,000 without salary sacrifice, then you can expect them to grow to £268,000 with salary sacrifice ... and so on.

These are significant increases. Remember this extra money is completely **free**! You would not have to save a single penny extra to enjoy this boost to your retirement savings.

The extra money comes about because you and your employer are saving national insurance.

Note, your *total* pension pot will not increase by 34%, just the amount that you were originally contributing personally. Remember John's employer was already contributing to his pension before the salary sacrifice took place. His employer's *original* (pre-salary sacrifice) contributions will not increase under a salary sacrifice arrangement.

How to Calculate Your Own Salary Sacrifice

Let's say you are a basic-rate taxpayer and personally contribute £100 to a pension. To get that £100 you will have had to earn salary of £147:

£147 _less_ 20% income tax _less_ 12% national insurance = £100

So if you give up £147 of salary *and* stop making pension contributions you will still have almost exactly the same amount of disposable income.

Therefore, to calculate how much salary to sacrifice, while keeping your disposable income the same, you simply take your net pension contribution and add back the 20% income tax and 12% national insurance you have paid.

To do this quickly, divide your net pension contribution by 0.68:

$$\frac{\text{Net Pension Contribution}}{0.68}$$

Example 1

John, as we know, is a basic-rate taxpayer and personally contributes £1,000 to his employer's pension plan annually (this is his net pension contribution). His total gross contribution, including the taxman's top up, is £1,250. The amount of salary John needs to sacrifice is:

$$£1,000/0.68 = £1,470$$

If John stops contributing to his pension plan and sacrifices this amount of salary, his disposable income will remain the same.

His employer will contribute £1,470 to his pension plan plus an extra £203 (£1,470 x 13.8%), representing the employer's national insurance saving. His total pension contribution will be £1,673 – an increase of £423 per year or 34%.

Example 2

Richard is a basic-rate taxpayer and personally contributes £3,000 to his employer's pension plan annually (this is his net pension contribution). His total gross contribution, including the taxman's top up, is £3,750. The amount of salary Richard needs to sacrifice is calculated as follows:

$$£3,000/0.68 = £4,412$$

If Richard stops contributing to his pension plan and sacrifices this amount of salary, his disposable income will remain the same.

His employer will contribute £4,412 to his pension plan plus an extra £609 (£4,412 x 13.8%), representing the employer's national insurance saving. His total pension contribution will be £5,021 – an increase of £1,271 per year or 34%.

Chapter 25

Salary Sacrifice Case Study: Higher-Rate Taxpayer

Introduction

In this chapter we are going to follow the same Jane from Chapter 23 and show how she can boost her pension pot with a salary sacrifice arrangement.

Remember, Jane earns £60,000 and is a higher-rate taxpayer. Higher-rate taxpayers pay 40% income tax and 2% national insurance on their earnings over £45,000 (£43,000 in Scotland).

Jane's Retirement Savings

We know from Chapter 23 that Jane's income tax and national insurance bill comes to £17,420.

Let's say she also personally contributes £2,400 into her employer's pension scheme. Her employer pays the amount to the pension scheme provider who in turn reclaims £600 of basic-rate tax relief from HMRC and credits this to Jane's pension pot, bringing her total pension contribution to £3,000.

Jane also receives a £600 income tax refund when she submits her tax return (her higher-rate tax relief).

(The assumption here is that the pension scheme uses the 'relief at source' method rather than the 'net pay' method – see Chapter 2.)

The company Jane works for also makes an employer contribution into her pension plan. Although this is most welcome, we will ignore this contribution and focus on Jane's own contributions.

After deducting her taxes and pension contribution and adding back her higher-rate tax relief, Jane is left with disposable income of £40,780: £60,000 - £17,420 - £2,400 + £600.

Avoiding National Insurance

So far Jane has enjoyed full *income tax* relief on her pension contributions but no national insurance relief because, as we know, there is no national insurance relief for pension contributions made by employees.

So Jane decides to stop contributing personally and asks her employer to make the contributions directly. In return, Jane agrees to sacrifice £3,103 of salary which takes her from £60,000 to £56,897 – I'll explain why she sacrifices this exact amount shortly.

After deducting income tax and national insurance she is left with £40,780 – the exact amount of disposable income she had before.

Jane's employer pays the £3,103 of sacrificed salary directly into her pension plan. Her employer also contributes the employer's national insurance saving, which comes to £428 (£3,103 x 13.8%).

Jane's pension contribution is now £3,531 and has increased by 18%.

It's not as much as the 34% increase enjoyed by John, the basic-rate taxpayer, because higher-rate taxpayers generally only save 2% national insurance on the salary they sacrifice, whereas basic-rate taxpayers save 12%.

Both types of taxpayer, however, can benefit from their employers' 13.8% national insurance saving.

It is also important to remember that Jane is enjoying much more *income tax* relief than John (40% as opposed to 20%).

In summary, Jane is enjoying 40% income tax relief, 2% employee's national insurance relief and 13.8% employer's national insurance relief on the money she contributes to her pension plan.

A summary of the number crunching is contained on the next page.

Jane's Take Home Pay Stays the Same

	Before Salary Sacrifice £	After Salary Sacrifice £
Salary	60,000	56,897
Less:		
Income tax	12,100*	11,459
National insurance	4,720	4,658
Pension contribution	2,400	0
Disposable income	**40,780**	**40,780**

... But Her Pension Contribution Increases By 18%

	Before Salary Sacrifice £	After Salary Sacrifice £
Employee contribution	2,400	-
Taxman's top up	600	-
Extra employer contribution	-	3,103
Employer's NI saving	-	428
Total	**3,000**	**3,531**

* Reduced by £600 higher-rate income tax relief.

18% –The Magic Number!

Although this is just a one-year snapshot, what we can deduce from this simple example is that higher-rate taxpayers who use salary sacrifice can boost their pension contributions by 18%.

This means salary sacrifice could have a significant impact on the amount of money you are able to save for retirement.

For example, if you would expect your own pension contributions to eventually grow in value to £100,000 without salary sacrifice, then you can expect them to grow to £118,000 with salary sacrifice.

If you would expect your own pension contributions to grow in value to £200,000 without salary sacrifice, then you can expect them to grow to £236,000 with salary sacrifice ... and so on.

These are significant increases. Remember this extra money is completely **free**! You would not have to save a single penny extra to enjoy this boost to your retirement savings.

The extra money comes about because you and your employer are saving national insurance.

Note, your *total* pension pot will not increase by 18%, just the amount that you were originally contributing personally. Remember Jane's employer was already contributing to her pension before the salary sacrifice took place. Her employer's *original* (pre-salary sacrifice) contributions will not increase under a salary sacrifice arrangement.

How to Calculate Your Own Salary Sacrifice

Let's say you are a higher-rate taxpayer and personally contribute £100 to your pension. The gross contribution is £125 (£100/0.8) and you will receive £25 of higher-rate relief (£125 x 20%). So the actual cost to you is just £75 (£100 - £25).

To get £75 of income in your hands you will have had to earn £129 of salary:

£129 *less* 40% income tax *less* 2% national insurance = £75

So if you sacrifice £129 of salary and stop making pension contributions you will still have the same amount of disposable income to spend.

To perform the same calculation for yourself and calculate how much salary you need to sacrifice just follow these two simple steps:

- **Step 1.** Multiply the amount you personally contribute to your pension by 0.75 – the resulting number is what your pension contributions are actually costing you and takes into account your higher-rate relief.

- **Step 2.** Add back the 40% income tax and 2% national insurance you have paid on this income. To do this divide the result from Step 1 by 0.58:

$$\frac{Step\ 1}{0.58}$$

Example

As we know, Jane is a higher-rate taxpayer and personally contributes £2,400 to her pension. The taxman tops this up with £600, so her gross pension contribution is £3,000. Jane's salary sacrifice is calculated as follows:

- ***Step 1.*** *Multiply the amount she personally contributes to her pension by 0.75:*

    £2,400 x 0.75 = £1,800

- ***Step 2.*** *Add back her 40% income tax and 2% national insurance by dividing the result by 0.58:*

    £1,800/0.58 = £3,103

If she sacrifices £3,103 of salary and stops contributing to her pension plan, her disposable income will remain the same.

Her employer will contribute £3,103 to her pension plan, plus an extra £428 (£3,103 x 13.8%). This is the employer's national insurance saving. Her total pension contribution will now be £3,531.

It's important to remember that she can enjoy this free increase to her pension pot **every year.**

Furthermore, this is just her national insurance saving. As a higher-rate taxpayer she will also be enjoying 40% income tax relief on her pension contributions.

A higher-rate taxpayer who personally contributes £2,400 to a pension plan will receive a £600 income tax refund from the taxman so the actual cost is just £1,800. The taxman's top-up will take the total pension contribution to £3,000.

With salary sacrifice the pension contribution then goes up to £3,531 without costing a penny extra.

Chapter 26

How to Convince Your Employer

After over 20 years in the tax publishing business one thing I have learnt is that most tax breaks come with a catch.

With salary sacrifice pensions the catch is you need your employer's co-operation. If your employer isn't already offering a salary sacrifice arrangement, you'll have to get him to agree to it and to do the necessary paperwork (see Chapter 28).

How much bargaining power you have with your employer will, of course, depend on how big the company is and how senior you are.

If you are a senior executive at a small or medium-sized company, you should find it relatively easy to get your employer to introduce a salary sacrifice arrangement. If you are a junior employee at a multinational corporation your chances are probably slim.

However, because a salary sacrifice arrangement could increase your pension pot by thousands of pounds, I believe it's worth fighting for tooth and nail.

Fortunately, there are several arguments you can use to convince your employer:

Argument #1 Other Employers Are Doing It

Salary sacrifice pensions are available from some of the country's biggest and most reputable companies, universities and other organisations, including BT, Tesco and the BBC.

To stay competitive in the jobs market your employer should also be offering this benefit.

Argument #2 Easy to Implement

As we will see in Chapter 28, the paperwork is relatively straightforward and may only have to be done once. Having said this, some employers may shy away from introducing a salary sacrifice arrangement if they are currently grappling with their new auto-enrolment duties and if they fear that a salary sacrifice pension arrangement will not be auto-enrolment compliant.

Argument #3 Giving Employees a FREE Pay Increase

This is by far the most powerful argument you can use to convince your employer to introduce a salary sacrifice pension arrangement.

The employee effectively receives a pay increase that doesn't cost the employer anything. The taxman foots the entire bill.

What rational employer would turn down such an opportunity?

Sharing the Savings with Your Employer

If you are struggling to convince your employer to introduce a salary sacrifice pension arrangement, you can offer to share the national insurance savings.

Remember there are two types of national insurance: the type the employee pays and the type the employer pays.

In all the examples so far we have assumed that both the employee's and employer's national insurance savings are paid into the employee's pension plan.

However, to convince your employer to introduce a salary sacrifice pension arrangement you may have to appeal to his selfish side and offer to share the national insurance savings.

Your employer generally pays 13.8% national insurance on every pound you earn over £8,164 (2017/18 figures). It may be necessary to offer your employer, say, half of the employer's national insurance saving (6.9% of the salary sacrifice amount) to co-operate with you.

Ideally you should negotiate to have your employer share the national insurance savings for just one year, perhaps to compensate him for time spent doing the necessary paperwork. However, even if your employer insists on a permanent national insurance share, you will still be far better off in most cases with a salary sacrifice pension arrangement.

For example, in Chapter 24 we showed how John, a basic-rate taxpayer, saw his pension contribution go up from £1,250 to £1,673 with a salary sacrifice arrangement – an increase of 34%. This was helped by his employer contributing his full national insurance saving of £203.

If his employer had only agreed to contribute half his saving John's pension contribution would have increased from £1,250 to £1,571 – an increase of 26%. John is still significantly better off with a salary sacrifice pension.

Similarly, in Chapter 25 we showed how Jane, a higher-rate taxpayer, saw her pension contribution go up from £3,000 to £3,531 with a salary sacrifice arrangement – an increase of 18%. This was helped by her employer contributing his full national insurance saving of £428.

If her employer had only agreed to contribute half his saving Jane's pension contribution would have increased from £3,000 to £3,317 – an increase of 11%. Jane is still better off with a salary sacrifice pension.

Employer Refuses to Share NI Savings

What happens if your employer refuses to share any of his national insurance savings? This is the worst-case scenario but cannot be ruled out.

If you are a basic-rate taxpayer a salary sacrifice pension may still be worth having because your pension contributions will still be approximately 18% higher.

If you are a higher-rate taxpayer, however, a salary sacrifice pension will increase your pension contributions by a paltry 3%. Remember, higher-rate taxpayers only pay 2% national insurance on earnings over £45,000. So a salary sacrifice saves them very little unless some or all of the employer's much larger 13.8% national insurance bill is also added to the pension pot.

In summary, a salary sacrifice arrangement loses most of its attractiveness if you are a higher-rate taxpayer and your employer refuses to share his national insurance savings.

When Your Employer Doesn't Pay NI

Most businesses currently receive an allowance of £3,000 per year to offset against their national insurance bills. Thus in some very small companies – those employing just one or two people on low salaries – there may be no employer's national insurance payable.

Employer's national insurance is also not payable for employees under the age of 21 and apprentices under 25 who are basic-rate taxpayers.

If the business doesn't have any national insurance to pay, a salary sacrifice will not produce an employer's national insurance saving that can be paid into the employees' pensions.

Summary

- Salary sacrifice requires your employer's approval.

- To convince your employer to introduce salary sacrifice you can use the following arguments:

    - Many big, reputable employers offer salary sacrifice
    - It is relatively easy to implement
    - It allows employers to provide FREE pay increases

- The national insurance savings can be shared with your employer. A basic-rate taxpayer could still end up with a 26% bigger pension pot. A higher-rate taxpayer could still end up with an 11% bigger pension pot.

- If your employer refuses to share any of his national insurance savings, a salary sacrifice arrangement is still worthwhile if you are a basic-rate taxpayer... but not very effective if you are a higher-rate taxpayer.

Chapter 27

Salary Sacrifice Drawbacks

With salary sacrifice your gross salary is reduced, so anything that depends on your gross salary could be affected, including your:

- Employment benefits
- Borrowing ability
- Maternity pay

For starters, the general consensus among pension experts is that you should not take part in a salary sacrifice arrangement if your income will fall below the lower earnings limit (currently £5,876).

This is because your entitlement to various state benefits may be affected if your income falls below the lower earnings limit, including state pension, statutory sick pay, maternity pay, incapacity benefit and jobseekers' allowance.

Also, your employer cannot let a salary sacrifice take you under the national minimum wage or national living wage.

Employment Benefits

If a salary sacrifice reduces your gross salary then this could *potentially* also reduce your:

- Future pay increases
- Overtime
- Life insurance cover provided by your employer
- Redundancy payments

Many salary sacrifice arrangements address this issue by making sure all benefits are based on the employee's original salary – often referred to as the reference salary, notional salary or base salary. So if you are currently earning £40,000 and your salary is reduced to £37,000, your employment benefits can be calculated on the basis that you are still earning £40,000.

Borrowing Ability

Any salary reduction could affect your ability to borrow money, for example to buy a house or for any other purpose.

One solution is for your employer to provide the lender with a letter of reference confirming your reference salary. For example, some of the university salary sacrifice documents state that:

"You should quote your current annual salary on mortgage applications and your payslip will substantiate this figure as your annual salary. If The University Payroll Office receives requests for mortgage references from lenders they will quote your current salary i.e. before the reduction."

This potential issue can therefore be addressed. However, there is still a potential risk that some lenders will not accept your reference salary and use the lower post-sacrifice salary.

New Single Tier State Pension

Since 6 April 2016 the basic state pension and state second pension have been replaced with a flat-rate pension currently worth £159.55 per week – £8,297 per year.

From now on your state pension entitlement is based solely on how many years of national insurance contributions or credits you have – the amount you earn is irrelevant.

Under the previous system your entitlement to the state second pension was based on your earnings and could therefore have been adversely affected by a salary sacrifice.

To qualify for the new state pension you need 35 years of national insurance contributions or credits – five years more than before. If you have less than 35 years you will get a proportion of the full state pension. For example, if you have 28 years of contributions you will get 80%.

To qualify for any state pension you will need a minimum level of contributions, usually 10 years worth. If you have less than this you will not receive any pension.

For those starting their working life after 5 April 2016, the new system is much simpler – you will simply get the flat–rate pension providing you have enough years of national insurance contributions.

If you were working before this date, your eventual state pension will be based on your previous national insurance record (the full value of your previous contributions will be preserved), and your current national insurance record since the switch to the new state pension.

Maternity Pay

A salary sacrifice arrangement could reduce the amount of statutory maternity pay (SMP) to which you are entitled. Statutory maternity pay is based on your contractual earnings which count for national insurance contributions. So if your earnings have been reduced because you sacrificed some salary, the amount of statutory maternity pay you receive may also be reduced.

If a salary sacrifice takes your salary below the lower earnings limit (£5,876 in 2016/17), you will lose your statutory maternity pay entitlement altogether.

How is Statutory Maternity Pay Calculated?

Women are entitled to 52 weeks of maternity leave and 39 weeks of statutory maternity pay.

For the first six weeks you are entitled to receive 90% of your average gross weekly earnings, with no upper limit. So a salary sacrifice could reduce the amount of SMP you receive for the first six weeks.

For the remaining 33 weeks you are entitled to receive the *lesser* of:

- £140.98 per week
- 90% of your average earnings

All except the lowest paid will receive a flat amount of £140.98 per week for this 33-week period, so a salary sacrifice will probably have no effect on this part of your SMP entitlement.

Statutory Maternity Pay – Effect on the Employer

Employers are liable to pay statutory maternity pay but can get most of it refunded.

If the employer's total payments of class 1 national insurance are £45,000 or less he can recover 103% of the SMP paid.

The extra amount is to compensate him for the employer's national insurance payable on the SMP.

If the employer's total class 1 national insurance payments are more than £45,000 per year, the employer can recover 92% of the SMP paid.

Employer vs Employee

With salary sacrifice pensions the idea is that neither the employee nor the employer ends up worse off. However, salary sacrifice pension arrangements could prove costly for employers when their staff are on parental leave.

The general rule is that employer pension contributions must continue to be made as normal while an employee is on paid parental leave. With salary sacrifice the employer's pension contributions are larger than normal so the cost could be higher.

There is also some debate as to whether salary sacrifice pension contributions must continue to be made during a period of unpaid parental leave.

Maternity Allowance

Maternity allowance is paid to women who are employed but not entitled to SMP. Maternity allowance is based on your earnings, so a salary sacrifice arrangement may reduce your entitlement to maternity allowance.

Chapter 28

How to Implement a Salary Sacrifice Pension

It is important to point out that salary sacrifice must be a *contractual agreement*, not an informal arrangement between you and your employer.

In other words, you have to change your employment contract and this should to be done in writing.

It may be possible to change your contract of employment by using a simple agreement letter, signed by both you and your employer. Many pension companies provide sample documents. This letter should be kept with your employment contract.

The new agreement must state what benefit is being received in exchange for the sacrificed salary.

It's important that the potential future salary is given up before it is treated as received for tax and national insurance purposes. Your terms of employment must be changed *before* the salary sacrifice commences.

HMRC is not against salary sacrifice but could challenge the arrangement if it has not been set up correctly and the paperwork is not in order.

Salary Sacrifice and Auto Enrolment

The operation of a salary sacrifice arrangement is separate from the automatic enrolment provisions (see Chapter 20), although the Pension Regulator states that employers can run the two in parallel when complying with their employer duties.

An employer can ask an employee who must be automatically enrolled whether they want to use a salary sacrifice arrangement. However, active membership of a pension scheme cannot depend on the employee agreeing to use salary sacrifice. If the employee does not agree to salary sacrifice, the employer must automatically enrol them into the pension scheme with an alternative method of making pension contributions.

The qualifying earnings used to work out the minimum pension contribution required under auto-enrolment are based on the post-sacrifice level of salary.

However, some commentators argue that it is better to base contributions on the pre-sacrificed salary to maintain good relations with employees.

Getting HMRC Approval

HM Revenue & Customs does not have to be notified of salary sacrifice arrangements. However, after the arrangement is set up employers can ask their local tax offices to confirm that the correct tax treatment is being applied.

HMRC will probably want to see evidence that the employment contracts have been changed correctly, and payslips, before and after the sacrifice.

Details can also be sent to:

HMRC Clearances Team
Alexander House
21 Victoria Avenue
Southend-on-Sea
SS99 1BD

Email: hmrc.southendteam@hmrc.gsi.gov.uk

This gives the employer reassurance the arrangement has been implemented correctly.

Payslips and P60s

Strictly speaking, your new post-salary-sacrifice payslip should not show your old salary, with the sacrificed amount shown as a deduction.

However, HMRC's guidance notes state that if the employment contract has been changed correctly, the payslip is less important.

However, if there are issues surrounding the employment contract, the payslip may be used to determine whether the salary sacrifice is valid.

HMRC recognises that some payroll software can only store one value for the employee's salary. This could create problems when calculating overtime and other benefits based on the higher pre-sacrifice reference salary.

However, as long as the contract has been modified correctly, and makes it clear that the employee is entitled to a reduced salary and specified benefits, HMRC should not invalidate the salary sacrifice.

HMRC's guidance notes point out that non-taxable benefits-in-kind must not be carried forward to the P60.

Finally, I would strongly recommend speaking to an advisor who has experience of salary sacrifice pensions and auto-enrolment before diving in and setting one up yourself.

Part 7

Company Directors

Chapter 29

Introduction

Company directors, just like regular employees, can contribute up to 100% of their 'relevant UK earnings' to a pension but typically not more than £40,000 (the annual allowance).

Your relevant UK earnings will include your:

- Salary and any bonus
- Taxable benefits in kind

For example, a company director with a salary of £20,000 can make a cash contribution of up to £16,000. The taxman will top this up with £4,000 of basic-rate tax relief for a gross pension contribution of £20,000.

A company director with a salary of £50,000 can make a cash contribution of up to £32,000. The taxman will top this up with £8,000 of basic-rate tax relief for a gross pension contribution of £40,000. He can make an additional pension contribution of £10,000 gross if he has unused annual allowance from any of the previous three years.

(Of course, as we saw in Chapter 3, the director may not want to make such a large contribution in practice because he would not receive higher-rate tax relief on the whole contribution.)

Company Pension Contributions

As a company owner you can also get your company (your employer) to make pension contributions on your behalf. Company pension contributions are always paid *gross* (there is no top up from the taxman) but the company will normally enjoy corporation tax relief on the payment.

For example, a company paying 19% corporation tax and making a pension contribution of £10,000 can claim corporation tax relief of £1,900 (£10,000 x 19%).

Pension contributions made by employers are not restricted by the level of the employee's earnings. A company pension contribution can be bigger than the director's earnings. However, there are other restrictions on company pension contributions:

Firstly, total pension contributions by you and your company must not exceed the £40,000 annual allowance, although any unused allowance from the previous three years can be carried forward and used to cover contributions made by both you and the company. (High income earners may be subject to a lower annual allowance – see Chapter 19.)

Secondly, the company may be denied corporation tax relief on any pension contributions made on behalf of directors, if the taxman views them as 'excessive'. We'll return to this point later.

In this part of the guide we explain why pension contributions are an attractive alternative to dividends, following the recent increase in dividend tax rates.

We also answer the important question asked by many company owners: "Who should make the pension contributions: me or the company?"

However, before doing that it's important to explain how company owners often structure their pay to reduce income tax.

Chapter 30

Salary or Dividend?

Most small company owners are both directors and shareholders. This means they can withdraw both salaries and dividends from their companies. Salaries are subject to income tax and national insurance, dividends are subject to income tax only.

Taking a big salary is generally not attractive because the national insurance cost is prohibitive. Up to 12% national insurance will have to be paid on a big chunk of the salary by the company owner personally and an extra 13.8% will usually have to be paid by the company.

But taking all the profits out as dividends is not the best solution for most small company owners either because this means subjecting all the company's profits to corporation tax (dividends are paid out of after-tax profits).

The optimal solution in many cases is to pay a small salary that is tax deductible in the company's hands and tax-free in the hands of the company owner.

What is the Optimal Tax-Free Salary for 2017/18?

There are two important income tax and national insurance thresholds for the current 2017/18 tax year:

- National insurance   £8,164
- Income tax   £11,500

For many company owners taking a salary equal to one of these thresholds is optimal.

In the chapters that follow we will assume that the company owner takes a salary of £8,164. A salary of £8,164 will not attract any employee's or employer's national insurance and, providing the company owner has no other income, will also be free from income tax.

Because salary payments are usually a tax deductible business expense, a salary of £8,164 could save the company at least £1,551 in corporation tax:

£8,164 x 19% corporation tax = £1,551

A salary of £8,164 will not be optimal for everyone, however.

For example, if your company does not use up its £3,000 national insurance employment allowance paying salaries to other employees, there may be spare employment allowance for the directors own salaries. In these circumstances a salary of up to £11,500 may be optimal.

Note that the employment allowance is no longer available to companies where a single director is the sole employee. According to HMRC guidance, the employment allowance also cannot be claimed if there are other employees BUT the director's salary is the only one on which employer's national insurance is payable. Many tax experts disagree with HMRC's interpretation of the rules.

There are many other tax and non-tax factors that may influence your salary decision. Some company owners may wish to pay themselves a bigger salary because, although strictly speaking not "optimal", this lets them take a bigger chunk of income out of the company on a regular basis, without some of the hassle that comes with paying dividends (for example, making sure the company has sufficient distributable profits and that dividends are properly declared).

For a complete discussion of this topic see the Taxcafe guide *Salary versus Dividends*.

Once they've paid themselves a small tax-free salary, many company owners take the rest of their income as dividends.

How Dividends Are Taxed

Dividends are subject to income tax but not national insurance. Also, the income tax rates on dividends are lower than the income tax rates on salaries because dividends are paid out of a company's *after-tax* profits: the money has already been taxed in the company's hands, whereas salaries are a tax deductible expense.

The tax treatment of dividends has been completely changed with effect from 6 April 2016.

Dividend tax credits have been abolished, so it is no longer necessary to gross up your cash dividends to calculate your tax. All tax calculations now work with cash dividends only and are therefore a lot simpler.

(I generally refer to the amount of dividend actually paid, or deemed to be paid, as the "cash" dividend. This does not necessarily mean that it is literally paid in cash, as dividends are sometimes paid by way of accounting entries.)

While simpler tax calculations are the good news, the bad news is that new tax rates for cash dividends have been introduced that are 7.5% higher than the previous ones.

The first £5,000 of dividend income you receive is, however, tax free thanks to the "dividend nil rate band", also known as the "dividend allowance". Unfortunately, the dividend allowance is expected to fall to £2,000 in 2018/19.

For those receiving dividends in excess of the dividend allowance, the following income tax rates now apply (the old effective rates are included for comparison):

	Old	**Current**
Basic-rate taxpayers	0%	7.5%
Higher-rate taxpayers	25%	32.5%
Additional-rate taxpayers	30.6%	38.1%

Overall Tax Rates on Dividend Income

Because income paid as dividends is taxed twice (first in the hands of the company and second in the hands of the shareholder) it's easy to lose sight of how much tax is being paid overall.

As a company owner you are likely to be equally concerned about your company's tax bill as your own, so it's worth showing the overall combined tax rate on dividend income. With companies currently paying 19% corporation tax, the total tax rates on dividend income are as follows:

	Total Tax Rate
Basic-rate taxpayers	25%
Higher-rate taxpayers	45%
Additional-rate taxpayers	50%

A company with £100 of profit will pay £19 corporation tax, leaving £81 to pay as dividends. Ignoring the £5,000 dividend allowance, a higher-rate taxpayer will pay £26 tax on this income (£81 x 32.5%), so the total tax on the £100 profit is £45, i.e. 45%.

The above tax rates are significantly higher than the regular income tax rates that apply to most types of income (20% for basic-rate taxpayers, 40% for higher-rate taxpayers and 45% for additional-rate taxpayers).

This is because the Government wants to level the playing field between company owners (who often don't pay any national insurance) and self-employed business owners and regular employees, who pay national insurance on most of their earnings.

From a tax planning perspective, once they've used up the £5,000 dividend allowance, company owners may now be better off paying themselves certain types of income that are taxed at "regular" income tax rates in preference to dividends, wherever possible. An obvious example would be rental income (but not salary income if national insurance is also payable).

Finally, please note that I am not recommending that you structure your pay in the way described in this chapter. You should always speak to an accountant about your own optimal pay structure.

Chapter 31

Pension Contributions: Better than Dividends?

Following the increase in dividend tax rates, some company owners will probably start paying themselves smaller dividends and get their companies to make pension contributions instead.

There are several reasons why pension contributions are attractive:

- Like salaries, company pension contributions enjoy corporation tax relief. In other words, they're a tax deductible business expense.

- When you eventually withdraw money from your pension, 25% can be taken tax free.

- There is no national insurance on pension income.

- Pension income is taxed at the "regular" income tax rates, typically 20% or 40%. By contrast, the combined tax rate (corporation tax and income tax) on dividend income is currently 25% for basic-rate taxpayers and 45% for higher-rate taxpayers.

- When you start withdrawing money from your pension, you could find yourself in a lower tax bracket than you are now (most retirees are basic-rate taxpayers).

Putting all this together, there's a strong possibility that you will pay tax on your pension income at an effective rate of just 15% (and possibly lower), compared with the 25% or 45% you are currently paying on your dividend income.

There is, of course, a major drawback with pensions: your money is locked away until you are 55 (rising to 57 in 2028). Nevertheless, when you do reach the minimum retirement age, you can now make unlimited withdrawals.

Example – Higher-rate Taxpayer

Lesleyanne is a company owner and a higher-rate taxpayer.

Let's say she is trying to choose between taking an additional £100 of the company's profit as a dividend or getting the company to invest £100 in her self-invested personal pension (SIPP).

With a dividend the company will pay 19% corporation tax, leaving £81 to distribute. After paying income tax at 32.5% Lesleyanne will be left with around £55. The total tax rate will be roughly 45%.

A company pension contribution will enjoy corporation tax relief so the whole £100 will go straight into Lesleyanne's SIPP. Ignoring investment growth (it doesn't affect the outcome), when she eventually withdraws the money from her pension the first £25 will be tax free and the remaining £75 will subject to income tax.

If Lesleyanne is a basic-rate taxpayer when she retires she will pay 20% tax (£15), leaving her with £85. Thus her effective tax rate will be 15%.

If Lesleyanne is a higher-rate taxpayer when she retires (for example, if she ends up with a significant amount of other assets such as buy-to-let properties) she will effectively pay 40% tax on her taxable pension income (£30), leaving her with £70 overall. Thus her effective tax rate will be 30%, which is still better than the 45% currently payable on her dividend income.

It's also possible that some of Lesleyanne's pension withdrawals will be tax free thanks to her income tax personal allowance. In that case her effective tax rate will be 0%!

This example shows that, for company owners who have not already built up significant pension savings, a company pension contribution is an extremely attractive alternative to additional dividend income.

Of course, one must never lose sight of the fact that your pension savings are placed in a locked box until you are at least 55. So a company pension contribution is only an attractive alternative to a dividend if you have already withdrawn enough money from your company to cover your living costs.

In the previous example the company owner got her company to make a pension contribution to avoid the 32.5% tax payable on dividend income. But are company pension contributions worth making if you're a basic-rate taxpayer? Let's find out:

Example – Basic-rate Taxpayer

Poppy is a company owner and a basic-rate taxpayer.

She too is trying to choose between taking £100 of the company's profit as a dividend and a £100 company pension contribution.

With a dividend the company will pay 19% corporation tax, leaving £81 to distribute as a dividend. After paying income tax at 7.5% Poppy will be left with around £75. The total tax rate will be roughly 25%.

With a company pension contribution the whole £100 will go straight into Poppy's SIPP. Ignoring investment growth, when Poppy eventually withdraws the money from her pension the first £25 will be tax free and the remaining £75 will subject to income tax.

Like Lesleyanne, the effective tax rate on her pension income will be:

- *0% if covered by her personal allowance*
- *15% if she is a basic-rate taxpayer*
- *30% if she is a higher-rate taxpayer*

Once again, if Poppy has enough income to cover her living costs, a company pension contribution is an extremely attractive alternative to additional dividend income... unless Poppy ends up wealthier in retirement and becomes a higher-rate taxpayer.

This could happen if, for example, she eventually inherits a significant amount of money and the investment income takes her over the higher-rate threshold.

If she expects to become a higher-rate taxpayer in the future she may be better off taking as much dividend income as she can taxed at just 7.5%, while she can, and investing the surplus funds in an ISA.

Future Changes to Corporation Tax

The corporation tax rate fell from 20% to 19% on 1 April 2017 and will fall again to 17% on 1 April 2020.

Dividends will become a bit more attractive if they're paid out of profits that have been taxed at 17% instead of 19% or 20%.

For example, when the corporation tax rate falls to 17% the total combined tax rate on dividends will fall from 25% to 23% (basic-rate taxpayers) and from 45% to 44% for higher-rate taxpayers.

The flipside is that companies will enjoy less corporation tax relief on their pension contributions and other expenses.

Calculating Corporation Tax Relief

To keep things simple in the above examples, I assumed that the company pays 19% corporation tax. However, if your company's current accounting period started *before* April 2017, it will have a slightly higher effective corporation tax rate and enjoy more tax relief on its pension contributions.

Example
Clova owns Corrie Fee Ltd which has an accounting period that runs from 1 August 2016 to 31 July 2017. In January 2017 the company made a £10,000 pension contribution into Clova's SIPP. Corrie Fee Ltd will pay corporation tax as follows:

- *8 months to 31 March 2017   20%*
- *4 months to 31 July 2017   19%*

Effectively the company will pay 20% corporation tax on approximately two thirds of its profits and 19% tax on one third of its profits. This means the company's effective corporation tax rate will be 19.67%.

Thus the £10,000 pension contribution will save the company £1,967 in corporation tax (£10,000 x 19.67%). If a similar pension contribution is made in January 2018, the company will enjoy 19% corporation tax relief (£1,900).

Auto-Enrolment

For several years now the Government has been rolling out a system of compulsory pensions called auto-enrolment. Essentially it's an extra tax on employers.

Only employees earning more than £10,000 and aged from 22 to state pension age need to be *automatically* enrolled into a pension. Some older and younger employees and those who earn less than £10,000 also have certain workplace pension rights.

According to the Pension Regulator a company does not have any automatic-enrolment duties when:

- It has just one director, with no other staff

- It has a number of directors, none of whom has an employment contract, with no other staff

- It has a number of directors, only one of whom has an employment contract, with no other staff

A contract of employment does not have to be in writing. However, according to the Pension Regulator, if there is no written contract of employment, or other evidence of an intention to create an employer/worker relationship between the company and the director, it will not argue that an employment contract exists.

If a director does not have an employment contract they are always exempt from automatic enrolment. If a director has a contract of employment and there are other people working for the company with an employment contract, they are not exempt.

Depending on their age and earnings, they may qualify for automatic enrolment but the company can decide whether to automatically enrol them into a pension. However, the director has the right to join a pension scheme at any time and the company cannot refuse to enrol them (although in practice this problem will not arise in most owner-managed companies).

If the company decides not to enrol any employed director who is eligible for automatic enrolment, and it has no other eligible staff, it does not need to set up a pension scheme. However, it will need to make a 'declaration of compliance'.

Chapter 32

Pension Contributions: You or the Company?

In the previous chapter we showed that company pension contributions can be an attractive alternative to dividends.

However, company directors can also make pension contributions *personally*, so a key question is:

"Who should make the contributions: the director or the company?"

Before the increase in dividend tax rates it was often more tax efficient for a small pension contribution to be made by the company director personally.

At present it is often tax efficient in most cases to get your company to make the pension contributions, although this may change in future when the corporation tax rate is reduced further.

Company Owner Pension Contributions

As we know from previous chapters, when you make pension contributions *personally* (as opposed to getting your company to make them) the taxman will top up your savings by paying cash directly into your pension. Effectively for every £80 you invest, the taxman will put in an extra £20.

Why £20? Your contributions are treated as having been paid out of income that has already been taxed at the 20% basic rate of income tax.

The company that manages your pension plan – usually an insurance company or SIPP provider – will claim this money for you from the taxman and credit it to your account.

So whatever contribution you make personally, divide it by 0.80 and you'll get the total amount that is invested in your pension pot (your gross pension contribution).

Example

Peter is a company owner who takes most of his income as dividends. He invests £800 in a self-invested personal pension (SIPP). The taxman will top up his pension with £200 of basic-rate tax relief which means he'll have £1,000 in his pension pot:

$$£800/0.80 = £1,000$$

If Peter is a higher-rate taxpayer he can also claim higher-rate tax relief when he completes his tax return. This is given by increasing his basic-rate band by the amount of his gross pension contribution.

Example continued

Peter's gross pension contribution is £1,000 so his basic-rate band will be increased by £1,000. This means £1,000 of his dividend income will be taxed at 7.5% instead of 32.5%, i.e. a 25% saving. Thus, Peter's higher-rate tax relief is:

$$£1,000 \times 25\% = £250$$

In total Peter will enjoy £450 of tax relief (£200 basic-rate relief plus £250 higher-rate tax relief). Peter's total tax relief is 45% of his £1,000 gross pension contribution.

Company Directors with Small Salaries

To obtain tax relief on your pension contributions they have to stay within certain limits:

- **Earnings**. Contributions made by you *personally* must not exceed your 'relevant UK earnings'. Earnings include your salary, bonus and taxable benefits in kind but do NOT include your dividends.

- **The £40,000 Annual Allowance.** Total pension contributions by you and your company must not exceed £40,000 per year, although it is possible to carry forward any unused annual allowance from the three previous tax years. The annual allowance is reduced if your "adjusted income" exceeds £150,000 (see Chapter 19).

For a company director taking the 'optimal' tax-free salary of £8,164, the maximum pension contribution that can be made in 2017/18 is therefore £8,164.

This is the maximum *gross* contribution. The director would personally invest £6,531 (£8,164 x 80%) and the taxman will top this up with £1,633 in basic-rate tax relief for a total gross contribution of £8,164.

For a company director taking a salary of £11,500, the maximum gross pension contribution is £11,500. The director would personally invest £9,200 (£11,500 x 80%) and the taxman will top this up with £2,300 in basic-rate tax relief for a total gross contribution of £11,500.

Directors who want to make bigger pension contributions personally have to pay themselves bigger salaries. However, this is usually not an attractive option because a bigger salary may be subject to both employee's and employer's national insurance (at 12% and 13.8% respectively).

Company Pension Contributions

As a company owner you can also get your company (your employer) to make pension contributions on your behalf. Company pension contributions are always paid *gross* (there is no top up from the taxman) but the company will normally enjoy corporation tax relief on the payment. For example, a company paying 19% corporation tax can make a pension contribution of £10,000 and enjoy £1,900 tax relief.

Note, you do not need a dedicated company pension scheme to make company pension contributions. Most firms that offer SIPPs have special forms that allow your company to pay directly into your pension (although these plans may not be qualifying schemes for auto-enrolment purposes).

How much can your company contribute? Unlike the contributions that you make personally, the company's contributions are NOT restricted by the size of your salary.

In other words, the company can make a pension contribution that is bigger than your salary.

However, there are other restrictions on company contributions:

- Total pension contributions by you and your company must not exceed annual allowance (typically £40,000), although you can carry forward any unused allowance from the previous three tax years.

- The company may be denied corporation tax relief on any pension contributions made on behalf of directors, if the taxman views them as 'excessive' (see below).

Corporation Tax Relief on Pension Contributions

Unlike the pension contributions that you make personally, tax relief for company pension contributions is not automatic.

Company contributions will only be a tax deductible expense for corporation tax purposes if they are incurred wholly and exclusively for the purposes of the trade.

There is a danger that HMRC will deny corporation tax relief for 'excessive' pension contributions. In practice this is relatively rare.

When determining whether company pension contributions qualify for corporation tax relief, HMRC will look at the total remuneration package of the director. The total package (including salary, pension contributions and other benefits in kind) must not be excessive relative to the work the individual carries out and his or her responsibilities.

Relevant factors may include:

- The number of hours you work, your experience and your level of responsibility in the company.

- The pay of other similar employees in your company and other companies.

- The pay required to recruit someone to take over your duties.

- The company's financial performance.

Extra care may be necessary in the event of a large one-off company pension contribution.

It may be sensible to document the commercial justification (e.g. strong recent financial performance of the company) in the minutes of a directors' board meeting and hold a shareholders' meeting to approve the contribution.

In some cases, when a much larger than normal contribution is made, it may be necessary to spread tax relief over a number of years. These spreading rules will not affect most small companies and only kick in when the excess contributions amount to £500,000 or more.

Although the risk that your company will be denied corporation tax relief may be small, it is important to stress that, when it comes to company pension contributions, unlike contributions made by individuals, there is no cast-iron guarantee that the company will enjoy tax relief.

That's why I would recommend speaking to a tax advisor before your company starts making significant contributions.

Pension Contributions – You or the Company?

Using a couple of case studies we will now compare company pension contributions with pension contributions made personally by company owners to see which is most tax efficient.

Case Study 1 – Basic-rate Taxpayer

Eva owns Cassidy Ltd. She is a basic-rate taxpayer and pays herself a small tax-free salary of £8,164 and takes the rest of her income as dividends.

In 2017/18 she decides to make a £1,000 pension contribution. If Cassidy Ltd makes the contribution it can pay £1,000 directly into Eva's SIPP.

If instead Eva pays herself a dividend to fund a pension contribution that she makes personally the company will pay 19% corporation tax leaving Eva with £810.

Eva holds onto £10 and invests £800 in her SIPP. The taxman will add £200 of basic-rate tax relief, leaving her with the same amount in her pension – £1,000.

But that's not the end of the matter: Eva will still have to pay 7.5% tax on her £810 dividend – roughly £60.

Eva is worse of by about £50 (£60 - £10 of saved dividend income).

Thus, if you're a basic-rate taxpayer, for every £1,000 that ends up in your pension you will have to pay an additional 5% in tax.

In this case a company pension contribution is clearly more tax efficient than a contribution made personally by the director.

Other Important Points

If Eva wants more than £8,164 invested in her pension, making the contribution personally will be even more expensive.

She would have to pay herself a bigger salary and this could result in a significant amount of national insurance becoming payable. This is because any pension contribution you make personally cannot exceed your earnings (i.e. salary).

The additional salary would attract 12% employee's national insurance and 13.8% employer's national insurance (unless there is spare employment allowance).

Case Study 2 – Higher-rate Taxpayer

This time we'll assume Eva is a *higher-rate taxpayer* and again wants to make a £1,000 pension contribution.

If Cassidy Ltd makes the contribution it can pay £1,000 directly into Eva's SIPP. Alternatively Eva can pay herself an £810 dividend, hold onto £10 and invest £800 in her SIPP. The taxman will add £200 of basic-rate tax relief, resulting in the same gross pension contribution of £1,000.

Again, that's not the end of the matter. Eva still has to pay income tax on the additional dividend.

With a gross pension contribution of £1,000, Eva's basic-rate band will be increased by £1,000. This means the £810 dividend will be taxed at just 7.5%, not 32.5%, so the tax is roughly £60.

Furthermore, an additional £190 of her other dividend income will also be taxed at 7.5% instead of 32.5%, saving her an extra £48.

All in all a £1,000 pension contribution made by the director is only £2 more expensive than a contribution made by the company:

£60 income tax - £48 higher-rate relief - £10 saved dividend = £2

In this case a company pension contribution is again more tax efficient than a contribution made personally by the director but the difference is tiny.

Because the saving is so small it will probably be other factors that determine whether the company or the individual makes the pension contributions.

The small penalty for making pension contributions personally will be reversed when the corporation tax rate is reduced to 17% – i.e. it may then become slightly more tax efficient to make pension contributions personally if you are a higher-rate taxpayer.

Other Important Points

Note that if Eva wants to enjoy full higher-rate tax relief on a gross pension contribution of £8,164 (i.e. equal to her salary), she must have at least £8,164 of dividend income above the higher-rate threshold (income of at least £53,164 in 2017/18).

If Eva wants to make a pension contribution bigger than £8,164 personally she will have to pay herself a bigger salary and this may result in a significant amount of national insurance becoming payable.

Lifetime ISA versus Company Pension Contribution

In Chapter 14 we examined the new Lifetime ISA. Like pensions they attract a top up from the Government but, unlike pensions, ALL the money you take out will be tax free.

Let's say a company owner who is a basic-rate taxpayer is trying to decide between a £1,000 company pension contribution and using a dividend to fund a Lifetime ISA contribution.

A £1,000 pension contribution will attract corporation tax relief so the whole £1,000 will go directly into the company owner's pension.

If the same money is used to fund a dividend, the company will pay 19% corporation tax leaving £810 to pay out. After paying 7.5% income tax the company owner will be left with around £750 to invest in a Lifetime ISA. Adding the Government bonus the company owner will end up with £938 in his Lifetime ISA.

However, when the company owner retires all withdrawals from the Lifetime ISA will be tax free, whereas only 25% of the money withdrawn from the pension will be tax free. The rest will be taxed at 20% if he is a basic-rate taxpayer.

If we ignore investment growth to keep the example simple (it doesn't affect the outcome), with a Lifetime ISA the company owner will end up with £938, with a pension he will end up with just £850 after tax.

Thus, if you're a basic-rate taxpayer, your retirement income could be 10.3% higher with a <u>Lifetime ISA</u>!

What about higher-rate taxpayers? Once again a £1,000 pension contribution will attract corporation tax relief so the whole £1,000 will go directly into the company owner's pension.

If the same money is used to fund a dividend, the company will pay 19% corporation tax leaving £810 to pay out. After paying 32.5% income tax the company owner will be left with £547 to invest in his Lifetime ISA. Adding the Government bonus the company owner will end up with £684 in his Lifetime ISA.

When the company owner retires all withdrawals from the Lifetime ISA will be tax free, whereas only 25% of the money withdrawn from the pension will be tax free. The rest will be taxed at 20% if he is now a basic-rate taxpayer (most retirees end up as basic-rate taxpayers).

Ignoring investment growth again, with a Lifetime ISA the company owner will end up with £684, with a pension he will end up with £850 after tax.

Thus, your retirement income could be 24% higher with a _pension_.

However, if the company owner is a higher-rate taxpayer when he retires (e.g. if he has a lot of income from other sources, e.g. rental property) he will end up with £700 from a pension, compared with £684 from a Lifetime ISA. The difference is small and the investment decision will probably be based on other factors.

Summary

- Company pension contributions are currently more tax efficient than contributions made personally by directors.

- The additional saving is very small if the director is a higher-rate taxpayer and will be reversed when the corporation tax rate is reduced to 17%.

- However, if you want to make a pension contribution bigger than your existing company salary it is usually more tax efficient to get the company to make the contribution rather than pay yourself a bigger salary which may have a significant national insurance cost.

- Tax relief for company pension contributions is not automatic – tax relief could be denied if the contributions are viewed as excessive, although this is rare in practice.

- A Lifetime ISA is an attractive alternative to a company pension contribution if you are a basic-rate taxpayer, although you can only invest £4,000 per year and must be under 40 to open one. Pension contributions may be a more attractive alternative if you are a higher-rate taxpayer.

Part 8

The Self Employed & Property Investors

Chapter 33

Pension Planning for the Self Employed

The number of self-employed business owners saving for retirement has fallen dramatically in recent years.

Back in the 1990s around 60% were contributing to a pension. Today the figure is closer to 20%.

When HMRC uses the term 'self employed' they are referring specifically to owners of unincorporated businesses, ie sole traders and partnerships. Most company owners are classified as employees (see Part 7 for more on company owners).

Most of the chapters in this guide are relevant for self-employed individuals. However, there are a few additional points that need to be made.

In particular, to maximise the tax relief on your pension contributions it is important to know how much taxable income you have. Most regular employees know how much taxable income they have: all they have to do is look at their payslips!

Many company owners also know how much taxable income they earn *personally*. The *company's* profits may fluctuate from year to year but many directors know how much salary or dividend income they are going to withdraw.

The taxable income of self-employed business owners is often much harder to predict. Taxable income for these individuals is normally the pre-tax profits of the business and there could be significant swings from year to year.

For example, a big order before the end of the tax year could increase taxable profits significantly. Several months of poor trading conditions could see profits fall sharply or even produce a loss for the year.

Sometimes it's not just the sales of the business that will result in big changes to taxable income. The business owner may deliberately drive down taxable profits, for example by making investments in tax-deductible equipment (e.g. vans or computers).

So what has all this got to do with maximising tax relief on pension contributions?

Well for starters, in Chapter 2 we pointed out that to enjoy any tax relief on your pension contributions you must have 'relevant UK earnings'. If your business makes a loss you won't have any earnings and the maximum pension contribution you can make is £3,600 (the 'universal pension contribution' that everyone under age 75 can make).

In Chapter 3 we pointed out that to maximise your higher-rate tax relief, your gross pension contributions should not exceed the amount of income you have over the higher-rate threshold (£45,000 in most parts of the UK, £43,000 in Scotland).

In other words, someone living in England with taxable income of £50,000, who wants to maximise their higher-rate tax relief, should make a gross pension contribution of no more than £5,000 (£50,000 – £45,000).

A sole trader with bumper profits of £85,000 may want to make a big catch-up pension contribution of, say, £40,000 but suspend contributions if taxable profits fall back to £45,000.

In Chapter 16 we discussed the pros and cons of postponing pension contributions if you are a temporary basic-rate taxpayer. For example, during tough economic times (or if the business has a lot of tax-deductible expenditure for the year) the business owner may become a basic-rate taxpayer and decide to postpone making pension contributions until he becomes a higher-rate taxpayer in a future tax year.

Finally, in Chapter 18 we explained why self-employed business owners may wish to make bigger than normal pension contributions during tax years in which their profits are £50,000 to £60,000, in order to avoid the child benefit tax charge.

Calculating Pre-tax Profits

Although many sole traders may want to vary the amount they contribute to a pension each year in order to maximise their tax relief, the problem for some is they don't know how much profit the business is making!

They may only have this information after they draw up their accounts for the year. This may happen many months after the tax year has ended – in other words, when it is too late to make pension contributions (remember you cannot make backdated pension contributions).

Example
Elliott is a sole trader with a 31 March year end.

On 5 April 2018 (the final day of the 2017/18 tax year) he makes a net cash pension contribution of £4,000. The taxman adds £1,000 of basic-rate tax relief for a gross pension contribution of £5,000. Elliott expects to have pre-tax profits of around £50,000 for 2017/18 and therefore expects to receive £1,000 of higher-rate tax relief (£5,000 x 20%).

Elliott's accountant finishes drawing up the accounts for the business in July 2018 and, after taking account of all of his tax-deductible expenditure, calculates that Elliott has pre-tax profits of £47,000.

This means Elliott will only enjoy higher-rate tax relief on £2,000 of his gross pension contribution (£47,000 - £45,000 higher-rate threshold), saving him just £400 in higher-rate tax (£2,000 x 20%). If Elliott had known that his profits would turn out to be £3,000 lower he may have held onto some of his cash and made a bigger pension contribution in a future tax year when his income was higher.

The problem for Elliott is he had just five days from the end of his business accounting period to the end of the tax year to calculate his pre-tax profits and make a pension contribution that produced the maximum amount of higher-rate tax relief.

Most business owners would find this difficult if not impossible to do and very few accountants would be prepared to work to such a tight deadline.

Some business owners have a 5 April year end and therefore no time at all to accurately calculate their pre-tax profits.

Uncertainty about the level of pre-tax profits is less of a problem for business owners who are confident their pre-tax profits will exceed the higher-rate threshold by a big margin, especially if their pension contributions are quite modest (for example, someone who reckons pre-tax profits will be £80,000 and wants to make a £5,000 pension contribution).

However, it could be a problem even for high earners if they want to make big catch-up pension contributions and want higher-rate tax relief on the lot (for example, someone who expects to make pre-tax profits of £85,000 and wants to make a £40,000 pension contribution).

Changing the Accounting Year End

One option is to change your accounting year end to a date other than the tax year.

For example, let's say the business year end is 30 April 2017. This year end falls into the 2017/18 tax year which means the business owner would have from 30 April 2017 until the end of the tax year on 5 April 2018 to draw up accounts and decide what level of pension contribution to make.

Changing your accounting date has other tax benefits and drawbacks. For more information see the Taxcafe guide, *Small Business Tax Saving Tactics*.

Chapter 34

Pension Planning for Property Investors

When I started out writing this guide, I planned to conduct a comprehensive study comparing pensions and buy-to-let property. However, I quickly abandoned this idea for two reasons.

Firstly, a pension is not an asset, it's simply a 'wrapper' that protects the underlying assets from tax. Those assets are normally shares and bonds and sometimes commercial property (but not residential property which is prohibited).

So any comparison between pensions and buy-to-let ultimately boils down to a comparison between stock market investing and residential property investing.

Plenty of academics have conducted studies to see which asset class performs best but the results are sensitive to the time period under consideration and, critically, whether you include rents and dividends in the analysis.

The second reason why I decided not to spend time comparing pensions and buy-to-let property is that many property investors would simply not countenance investing in anything else. "Nothing beats bricks and mortar," goes the popular mantra.

I've lost count of the number of times I've heard the phrase "my properties are my pension".

So what I've decided to do in this chapter is explore whether a pension can be used to *complement* an investment in buy-to-let property.

This is particularly important now that tax relief on mortgage interest is being reduced (from April 2017).

Many landlords will see their tax bills rise significantly but it may be possible to mitigate the effects by making pension contributions.

Changes to Mortgage Tax Relief

Tax relief for interest and finance costs paid by individual landlords who own residential properties is now being restricted.

The new rules do not apply to commercial properties or furnished holiday lettings or to properties held inside companies.

Tax relief is currently being phased out over a period of four years and replaced with a 20% basic-rate "tax reduction" as follows:

- 2017/18   75% deducted as normal, 25% at basic rate only
- 2018/19   50% deducted as normal, 50% at basic rate only
- 2019/20   25% deducted as normal, 75% at basic rate only
- 2020/21   All relieved at basic rate only from this year on

The reduced tax relief on mortgage interest means many landlords will have significantly bigger *taxable* rental profits, even if their true rental profits remain unchanged.

Using Pensions to Beat the Tax Increase

A simple way for landlords to beat the tax increase is by making pension contributions.

How much will you need to invest to claw back all the extra tax you'll pay? As a rule of thumb, your *gross* pension contribution will need to be half as big as your non-deductible interest.

So if you have £10,000 of buy-to-let interest in 2020/21, when the changes are fully phased in, you will typically need to make a gross pension contribution of £5,000 to recover the extra tax you will pay.

In the examples that follow we will assume that the Government keeps its promise to raise the personal allowance to £12,500 in 2020/21 and to raise the higher-rate threshold, where 40% tax kicks in, to £50,000.

The higher-rate threshold will probably be lower in Scotland and the examples that follow are based on the tax rates and thresholds that will apply in the rest of the UK.

Example – Before Pension Contribution

Let's say it's 2020/21 and Usman earns £40,000 as a self-employed consultant and a rental profit of £10,000 (after deducting £10,000 of buy-to-let interest) from some residential properties. If Usman's mortgage tax relief was NOT restricted he would have total taxable income of £50,000 and his total after-tax income would be:

£50,000 income - £7,500 tax = £42,500

However, with his mortgage interest no longer tax deductible, Usman's Income Tax bill will increase by £2,000 to £9,500 (he'll have an extra £10,000 taxed at 40% but will also be entitled to a 20% tax reduction). In summary, his after-tax income will fall from £42,500 to £40,500.

(Usman's National Insurance has been ignored for simplicity.)

Example – After Pension Contribution

Usman decides to invest £4,000 in his pension. The taxman will add £1,000 of basic-rate tax relief, giving him a gross pension contribution of £5,000. He will also receive higher-rate tax relief through his self-assessment tax computation. This is calculated as 20% of his gross pension contribution: £5,000 x 20% = £1,000.

In total Usman enjoys £2,000 tax relief by making a £5,000 gross pension contribution (a cash contribution of £4,000). Hence, all the extra tax arising due to the reduction in his interest relief is clawed back by making a gross pension contribution half as big as his mortgage interest payments.

Pensions: Cashflow Issues

Although you can completely reverse the tax increase by making pension contributions, there is one significant problem: your money is locked away until you reach the minimum retirement age (currently 55). In other words, pension contributions can seriously damage your cashflow!

We saw that Usman's disposable income will fall from £42,500 to £40,500 when his mortgage tax relief is fully restricted. By making a pension contribution he claws back £2,000 and ends up with £42,500 again BUT £5,000 of that is stuck inside a pension plan! His actual disposable income will fall by a further £3,000 to £37,500. Usman's financial position is summarised below:

Usman: Tax Relief versus Cash Flow

	No Pension Contribution	Pension Contribution
	£	£
Sole trader profit	40,000	40,000
Taxable rental profit	20,000	20,000
	---------	---------
	60,000	60,000
Less:		
Income tax	9,500[1]	8,500[2]
Pension contribution	0	4,000
Mortgage interest[3]	10,000	10,000
Disposable income[4]	**40,500**	**37,500**
Pension Pot	**0**	**5,000**

Notes
1. First £12,500 tax free, next £37,500 taxed at 20%, final £10,000 taxed at 40%. Reduced by £2,000 tax reduction (mortgage interest x 20%).
2. Further reduced by £1,000 higher-rate tax relief on pension contribution.
3. Taxable rental profit is not the same as actual rental profit; his £10,000 of mortgage interest must be deducted to calculate his true disposable income.
4. Ignores national insurance payments. These would be the same under both scenarios and hence do not alter the overall conclusion.

Why does Usman's disposable income fall by £3,000? Because he personally invests £4,000 into his pension but gets £1,000 of higher-rate tax relief back through his self-assessment tax computation.

In summary, when we get to 2020/21, for every £10,000 of mortgage interest you pay you will generally be able to claw back the extra tax you will face as a higher-rate taxpayer by making a £5,000 gross pension contribution. £3,000 will ultimately come from you and £2,000 from the taxman. Thus, your disposable income will also fall by a further £3,000.

Pension Contributions this Year (2017/18)

What about the current 2017/18 tax year? By how much do you have to increase your pension contributions to reverse the tax increase you will suffer now that one quarter of your interest is no longer tax deductible?

Example
Let's assume that in 2017/18 Usman has the same income and expenses as in the previous examples. With one quarter (£2,500) of his mortgage interest no longer tax deductible, his taxable income will increase from £50,000 to £52,500. His income tax bill will increase by £500 (he'll pay 40% tax on an extra £2,500 but will also be entitled to a 20% tax reduction).

Usman decides to invest £1,000 in his pension. The taxman will add £250 of basic-rate tax relief, giving him a gross pension contribution of £1,250. He will also receive higher-rate tax relief through his self-assessment tax computation. This is calculated as 20% of his gross pension contribution: £1,250 x 20% = £250.

In total, Usman enjoys £500 tax relief by making a £1,250 gross pension contribution (a cash contribution of £1,000).

Just as in the previous example all the extra tax arising due to the reduction in his interest relief is clawed back by making a gross pension contribution half as big as his non-deductible interest.

Once again Usman will have to remember that the money in his pension cannot be touched until he is at least 55.

Protecting Your Child Benefit

So far we've looked at the "bread and butter" case where the landlord is a regular higher-rate taxpayer and enjoys 40% tax relief on their pension contributions. Some landlords may be able to enjoy even more tax relief.

Take Usman, for example. His taxable income rises from £50,000 to £52,500 in 2017/18 and to £60,000 in 2020/21.

With income over £50,000 he will end up paying the child benefit charge if he is a parent and the highest earner in the household.

In this case a pension contribution will reduce his "adjusted net income" which will also reduce the child benefit charge.

For example, in 2020/21 his £5,000 gross pension contribution will reduce his adjusted net income from £60,000 to £55,000 which means his child benefit charge will be halved from around £2,500 to £1,250 (if he has three children, based on current rates). In total, Usman will enjoy £3,250 tax relief on his £5,000 pension contribution, i.e. 65% tax relief.

Other Important Tax Thresholds

If your taxable income gets pushed over the £100,000 tax threshold you will also start losing your personal allowance. This year, once your income reaches £123,000 your personal allowance will be completely withdrawn.

However, making pension contributions will reduce your adjusted net income which means you will also recover some of your personal allowance, as well as enjoying the regular pension tax reliefs.

As a result, making pension contributions while your income is in the £100,000-£123,000 tax bracket will generally attract 60% tax relief this year.

If your taxable income gets pushed over the £150,000 tax threshold this year you will start paying additional rate tax at 45%.

However, making pension contributions to claw back the extra tax may be more difficult for high income earners.

Your annual allowance (the maximum amount that can be invested in your pension) may be reduced if your "adjusted income" exceeds £150,000 – See Chapter 19 for more information.

As long as your contributions do not exceed your reduced annual allowance you will still receive full tax relief, up to 45%.

Postponing Pension Contributions

If you expect to be pushed into a higher tax bracket in a future tax year as the tax relief on your mortgage interest is reduced, should you postpone making any pension contributions so that you can enjoy more tax relief? An obvious example is a basic-rate taxpayer who expects to become a higher-rate taxpayer when less of their interest is tax deductible.

Example
During the current 2017/18 tax year Oswald has net rental income of £40,000 (after deducting his various costs except interest). His total interest payments are £20,000. He also has other taxable earnings of £20,000.

One quarter of his mortgage interest (£5,000) is no longer tax deductible so his taxable income will be £45,000 (£40,000 rental income - £15,000 interest + £20,000 other income).

Oswald will not be a higher-rate taxpayer in 2017/18 because his taxable income does not exceed the higher rate tax threshold of £45,000. If he makes any pension contributions in 2017/18 he will only enjoy basic-rate tax relief.

Now let's move forward to the 2020/21 tax year (when none of his mortgage interest will be tax deductible and the higher-rate threshold is expected to be £50,000). Oswald will now have taxable income of £60,000 which means he'll have £10,000 taxed at 40%.

This also means that if he makes a gross pension contribution of £10,000 he will enjoy 40% tax relief. If his household also receives child benefit then the pension contribution will also ensure that he does not pay the child benefit charge as well (assuming he is the highest earner in the household).

Should landlords postpone making pension contributions and build up some savings to make bigger than normal pension contributions several years from now when they will possibly enjoy at least twice as much tax relief?

In an ideal world the answer would be yes. However, with tax rules constantly changing there is no guarantee that you will enjoy more tax relief on your pension contributions in the future.

Many pension experts believe that higher-rate tax relief will eventually be abolished (apparently the Government wanted to do this before the EU referendum but backed down). If higher-rate tax relief will be abolished then higher-rate taxpayers should make the most of the existing rules while they can.

Basic-rate taxpayers arguably face less risk by postponing pension contributions until they become higher-rate taxpayers because any change is less likely to leave them worse off.

However, pension contributions should arguably never be postponed if this also means giving up contributions from your employer (which are essentially additional pay in a tax efficient form).

Do You Have Earnings?

Everyone under 75 can make a gross pension contribution of up to £3,600 per year.

If you want to contribute more your gross contributions must not exceed your annual earnings.

Salaries and trading profits are earnings for this purpose; rental profits generally are not. If a landlord wants to make big pension contributions he must have earnings from other sources.

Is Tax Only Deferred and Not Saved?

Subject to the 25% tax-free lump sum, withdrawals from your pension scheme will be taxable.

Arguably, therefore, your pension contributions are only deferring tax rather than saving it.

However, much of this depends on how you time your withdrawals and on what your income situation is at the time, so absolute savings are still possible if you get your timing right!

Chapter 35

Putting Property
into a Pension

Some business owners use a specialist SIPP or other pension plan to hold their business premises and in this chapter we'll take a look at the benefits and drawbacks.

Note that you can put *commercial property* into a pension but not residential property, so this option is not available to buy-to-let landlords.

Holding business property in a pension has a number of benefits:

- **Tax-free rent**. There is no income tax payable by you on the rent your business pays into your pension plan. These rent payments are also a tax deductible expense for the business.

- **No capital gains tax**. When a property held inside a pension is sold there is no capital gains tax payable.

- **Inheritance tax exemption**. Assets held in a pension fall outside your estate for inheritance tax purposes.

Although the ability to roll up rental income tax free inside a pension is enticing, you must never lose sight of the fact that all the money you eventually withdraw from your pension, over and above your 25% tax-free lump sum, will be subject to income tax.

If you are a higher-rate taxpayer at present but expect to be a basic-rate taxpayer when you retire (most retirees end up as basic-rate taxpayers), it's possible the rental income will ultimately be much less heavily taxed by going the pension route.

Similarly, although property held inside a pension can be sold without incurring capital gains tax, when you eventually withdraw the capital gain most of it (75%) will be subject to income tax.

If you are a basic-rate taxpayer when you retire you will pay 20% tax and if you are a higher-rate taxpayer you will pay 40% tax.

By contrast, if you sell commercial property that you own personally you will be subject to capital gains tax. Commercial property now benefits from the lower 20% CGT rate and it's possible some of the gain will be taxed at just 10% if your basic-rate band isn't used up by your other income. Some of the gain may also be covered by your annual exemption, currently £11,300.

In some cases a sale of business premises that you own personally will qualify for Entrepreneurs Relief. If so, a tax rate of 10% may apply to the whole gain, although this will generally not be the case if your company has paid you rent at a full commercial rate.

A property held inside a pension doesn't have to be sold when you retire. If your own business ceases to occupy the property it can be rented out to someone else who will pay rent to your pension which can roll up tax free.

Although property held inside your pension may fall outside your estate for inheritance tax purposes, in most cases the family members that inherit your pension pot will have to pay income tax on any money they subsequently withdraw, typically at 20% or 40%.

By contrast, if you own your business premises personally, the property may qualify for business property relief (100% if you are a sole trader, 50% if the business is used by your partnership or company).

Finally, when it comes to tucking away money inside a pension we must never lose sight of the fact that you will not be able to get your hands on any of the money until you are at least 55 (rising to 57 in 2028).

Clearly there are benefits to holding business property inside a pension but it is by no means a 'no brainer'. There are benefits but also drawbacks and each case would have to be decided on its merits with help from a professional.

Funding the Property Purchase

The purchase of a business property by a pension can be funded in several ways.

Typically you will use your existing pension savings, topped up with fresh contributions (including company pension contributions if you run a company).

It is also possible for your pension fund to borrow money but only up to 50% of its net assets. For example, if you have pension savings of £100,000 an additional £50,000 can be borrowed.

Some pension providers allow a part share in a property to be acquired by the pension plan, with the balance owned outside the pension.

Several individuals can also pool their pension savings to collectively buy a property.

Transferring Existing Property

If you already own the property you can sell it to your SIPP and this may allow you to release a sizeable amount of cash from your pension savings.

Properties have also been transferred into pensions as *in specie* pension contributions, with the member claiming income tax relief. Under this method a property worth, say, £100,000 would be transferred into the pension scheme with the pension scheme administrator claiming £25,000 of basic-rate tax relief to add to the member's pension pot and the member himself claiming up to £25,000 of higher-rate tax relief when he submitted his tax return.

In specie contributions are no longer permitted by many pension firms following a recent clamp down by HMRC because of perceived abuse.

Transferring an existing property into a pension is likely to result in capital gains tax becoming payable if the property has risen in value since you bought it.

As stated earlier, commercial property now benefits from the lower 20% CGT rate and some of the gain may be taxed at just 10% and some may be tax-free thanks to the annual exemption. It's unlikely that Entrepreneurs Relief would be available in such cases, however.

A sizeable capital gains tax bill may put off many existing property owners going down the pension route but others may still be tempted by the prospect of receiving a large cash payment out of their pension savings.

The transfer may also result in stamp duty land tax.

VAT may also be payable in certain circumstances but a refund can usually be claimed.

Costs and other Formalities

Not all pension providers deal with property purchases so you may need to transfer your existing pension savings to a specialist provider.

When your property is held inside a pension your business will have to be treated just like any other tenant, with no special favours, which means rent will have to be paid at a full market rate come hell or high water.

If rent is not paid this will be treated as an unauthorised payment by your SIPP and HMRC may levy a charge of 40% on you personally and a charge of up to 40% on the SIPP itself.

Property SIPPs are also much more expensive to run than those that only allow you to invest in traditional 'stocks and shares'.

Initial set up costs include legal fees, surveyor fees, lenders fees and fees to the pension company managing your SIPP.

Fees will have to be paid for regular rent revaluations and a third party property manager may have to be appointed to collect the rent from you.

Part 9
Family Pension Planning

Chapter 36

Couples: Who Should Make the Pension Contributions?

People without earnings (i.e. who don't work) can make a pension contribution of £2,880 per year. The taxman will add £720 of basic-rate tax relief, resulting in a gross pension contribution of £3,600.

Is this worth doing?

Some people think it is because, although there will only be basic-rate tax relief, the ultimate pension income may end up being completely tax free, covered by the individual's income tax personal allowance.

The broader question that needs answering is this:

Under what circumstances should you transfer money to a spouse or partner to make pension contributions?

We can answer this question with the aid of a case study.

Case Study

Rory is a higher-rate taxpayer and his wife Claire is either a basic-rate taxpayer or doesn't work at all (whichever you prefer). Rory contributes to a pension, Claire doesn't. The couple want to make additional pension contributions and are trying to decide *who* should make them.

Rory will enjoy higher-rate tax relief on his extra pension contributions BUT he expects to ultimately pay 20% income tax on his pension income. Claire will only enjoy basic-rate tax relief on her pension contributions BUT she hopes to pay 0% tax on her pension income (being fully covered by her personal allowance).

Let's assume the couple want to save an additional £2,880 annually. If Claire makes the contributions, the taxman will add £720 of basic-rate tax relief, producing a gross pension contribution of £3,600.

Rory can make a net cash contribution of £3,840. The taxman will add £960 of basic-rate relief, resulting in a gross contribution of £4,800. Rory will also receive £960 of higher-rate tax relief (£4,800 x 20%), so the net cost to him is also £2,880 (£3,840 - £960).

Every year Rory has an extra £4,800 going into his pension, whereas Claire only has £3,600.

If the money grows by 7% per year then after 20 years Rory's additional contributions will have grown to £210,553, whereas Claire will have £157,915.

In summary, Rory ends up with 33% more money than Claire... but this is no real surprise (see Chapter 16).

Withdrawing Income

Let's say they pass the minimum retirement age and decide to withdraw money from their pensions.

They can both take a 25% tax-free lump sum. The remaining 75% will be taxed when withdrawn.

Their positions are summarised in Table 7. The total after tax includes the tax-free lump sum and the income remaining after paying tax at either 0%, 20% or 40%.

For example, if Rory's additional contributions have grown £210,553 he will be able to take a tax-free lump sum of £52,638. If the remaining £157,915 is taxed at 20% he will be left with after-tax income of £126,332 – £178,970 in total.

Of course, Rory won't be able to withdraw the whole £157,915 in one tax year and pay just 20% tax – he will have to spread his withdrawals over several tax years.

The example is simplistic but does, nevertheless, offer some interesting insights.

Table 7
Couples Pension Planning
Who Should Make Contributions?

	Higher-rate relief on contributions	Basic-rate relief on contributions
	£	£
Total pension pot	210,553	157,915
25% Tax-free	52,638	39,479
75% Taxable	157,915	118,436
Total after tax:		
After-tax @ 0%	210,553	157,915
After-tax @ 20%	178,970	134,228
After-tax @ 40%	147,387	110,541

When Rory Should Make the Contributions

If Rory pays 20% income tax when he retires (remember he has other pension savings) he will end up with £178,970 eventually. If Claire pays 0% income tax (because she has no other pension savings and her pension withdrawals are covered by her income tax personal allowance over several tax years) she will end up with £157,915. Rory ends up with 13% more money.

So the first conclusion is this: Rory should keep on making the pension contributions, even if Claire's pension income will be tax free.

It's even more important that Rory makes the contributions if there is any likelihood that Claire will acquire another source of income (e.g. from rental properties, inherited assets, a business or job etc). If Claire ends up being taxed at 20% on her pension income she may end up with £134,228 to Rory's £178,970. Rory ends up with 33% more money in this scenario.

When Claire Should Make the Contributions

But what if Rory, like Claire, does not receive higher-rate tax relief on these additional pension contributions, only basic-rate tax relief? This would be the case if his existing pension contributions are already equal to the amount of income he has subject to higher-rate tax (see Chapter 3 for an explanation).

In this case Rory would end up with £134,228 to Claire's £157,915. Claire receives 18% more income in this scenario.

So the second conclusion is this: Claire should make the additional contributions if Rory cannot obtain any additional higher-rate tax relief and she expects to pay no tax on her pension income. It's a second-best outcome but may be the best route for some couples.

If Rory expects to be a higher-rate taxpayer when he retires (e.g. if he has a lot of other pension savings or taxable income) he could end up with £147,387. Claire will end up with £157,915 but only if she pays no tax on her pension withdrawals. If she pays 20% tax she will end up worse off than Rory, even though he pays 40% tax.

In most cases Claire only ends up better off than Rory if she pays 0% tax on her pension income. However, if she works she will eventually receive a taxable state pension which will probably use up a significant chunk of her personal allowance which means she will pay 20% tax on most of her other pension income.

Even if Claire has never worked she may receive some state pension. For example, she will build up state pension entitlement while she has children under 12 and qualifies for child benefit.

In these cases Claire may only be able to pay 0% tax on all her pension income if all her pension savings are withdrawn before she reaches state pension age. This may only be possible if she has a relatively small pension pot.

Less Common Scenarios

There are other permutations, including Rory paying 0% tax when he retires (the best-case scenario of all) and Claire paying 40% tax when she retires (the worst-case scenario of all) but these outcomes are less likely and will not be discussed further.

Avoiding the Child Benefit Charge

If Claire receives child benefit and Rory's taxable income is in the £50,000-£60,000 bracket, he should probably be the one making all the pension contributions.

This will allow him to reduce or avoid the child benefit tax charge and enjoy over 50% tax relief on his pension contributions (see Chapter 18).

Family Tax Planning and Other Issues

Finally, it's worth pointing out that Claire may have *non-tax* reasons for making pension contributions, for example if she feels this gives her greater financial security.

On this note it should be pointed out that there are other things the couple can do to make use of Claire's tax-free personal allowance before she receives any state pension. For example, rental properties and other assets could be placed in her name, as could money the couple may eventually inherit.

Lifetime ISAs

These are discussed in detail in Part 3. Those under 40 can save up to £4,000 per year in a Lifetime ISA with a £1,000 Government bonus.

If Claire is under 40 she may prefer to put her money into a Lifetime ISA instead of a pension because the upfront tax relief is the same BUT all her withdrawals will be completely tax free.

Similarly, if Rory expects to be a higher-rate taxpayer when he retires he may be better off investing his additional savings in a Lifetime ISA.

Chapter 37

Pensions for Children and Grandchildren

"When I was a boy of 14, my father was so ignorant I could hardly stand to have the old man around. But when I got to be 21, I was astonished at how much the old man had learned in seven years."
Mark Twain

Everyone under the age of 75 can make a pension contribution of £3,600 per year and receive basic-rate tax relief (which reduces the net cost to £2,880).

This means minor children can make pension contributions or, as is more likely in practice, their parents or grandparents can contribute on their behalf.

Many pension providers have special pension plans for minors, like the Junior SIPP from Hargreaves Lansdown. According to HM Revenue and Customs, around 60,000 children under 18 years of age are making use of this tax break.

Making pension contributions on behalf of a minor child could be a wonderful way to leave an asset of lasting value that cannot be frittered away, at least not until the child is a responsible adult!

These contributions have the added bonus of usually being exempt from inheritance tax, being covered by either the £3,000 annual inheritance tax exemption or the regular gifts out of income exemption.

Thanks to the magic of compound growth, a pension contribution made on behalf of a minor child could grow into a significant nest egg. For example, let's say you make 18 annual contributions of £2,880 starting in the year a child is born. Each contribution will be topped up with £720 of basic-rate tax relief (even though the child doesn't pay any income tax), producing a gross pension contribution of £3,600 per year.

If we assume that the investments in the pension grow by 7% per year, just before the child's 18th birthday, when the last contribution is made, the pension pot will be worth £122,397. However, that's not the end of the story. The money will continue to compound tax free until the child is at least 59 (the possible minimum retirement age). Just before the 59th birthday the money will have grown to £1.96 million.

Of course these figures aren't adjusted for inflation. If some inflation adjustments are made you still end up with a pension pot worth over £350,000 in today's money, which is still a tidy sum!

Junior ISAs

In 2011 a new savings vehicle, the Junior ISA, was introduced. Just like normal ISAs, money grows tax free but there is no upfront tax relief, as there is with pension contributions.

The annual investment limit is £4,128 for 2017/18.

Unlike regular ISAs, money cannot be withdrawn until the child reaches age 18. From that date the junior ISA becomes an adult ISA and the child can do what he or she likes with the money.

Junior SIPP vs Junior ISA

There's no doubt that most children or grandchildren would prefer you to contribute to a junior ISA instead of a junior SIPP. They will face big financial commitments between the age of 18 and 59, e.g. university fees, buying a home or raising children of their own.

However, there is also the risk that the child will fritter away all of that carefully saved up money, if they can access it at the tender age of 18.

Personally I prefer the pension route for the simple reason that your children or grandchildren are going to have to save for retirement anyway. In other words, they can never lose out with a pension but they can lose out with a junior ISA that is not spent wisely.

They'll thank you for it... one day!